CW00373651

About the Author

Writing with the authority of more than forty-five years of continous experience of higher conscious states, GOPI KRISHNA has provided the world with a literal treasure of writings and discourses on the vast subjects of consciousness and evolution. During the last twenty years of his life, Gopi Krishna devoted his energies to presenting the world with his ideas about the present world condition and the future evolution of the human race. By the time he passed away in July 1984 at the age of 81, he was acclaimed as a leading authority on the science of Kundalini and Consciousness Research.

Gopi Krishna's quest was to bring awareness and understanding of the dangerous situation that mankind is in at present. He believed that the race is in a continuing state of evolution, but has now reached a crucial stage in this development. Mankind is on the verge of a giant leap toward higher states of consciousness but at the same time has the knowledge and means to destroy himself and the planet at the push of a button.

He asserts that there are Divine Laws which are ruling our progress. The time has now come for mankind to understand these inviolable Laws and learn to live in harmony with his fellow human beings so that our evolution may proceed in a healthy way.

Also
Books by Gopi Krishna
in UBSPD

THE DIVINE POSSIBILITIES IN MAN

Gopi Krishna

UBSPD

UBS Publishers' Distributors Ltd.

New Delhi Bombay Bangalore Madras
Calcutta Patna Kanpur London

UBS Publishers' Distributors Ltd.
5 Ansari Road, New Delhi-110 002
Mumbai Bangalore Madras
Calcutta Patna Kanpur London

First Published   1993
Reprint   1996

Printed at Rajkamal Electric Press,
B-35/9 G.T. Karnal Road Industrial Area, Delhi-110 033

Religious Perspectives
ITS MEANING AND PURPOSE   vii

RELIGIOUS PERSPECTIVES
Its Meaning and Purpose

RELIGIOUS PERSPECTIVES REPRESENTS A QUEST for the rediscovery of man. It constitutes an effort to define man's search for the essence of being in order that he may have a knowledge of goals. It is an endeavor to show that there is no possibility of achieving an understanding of man's total nature on the basis of phenomena known by the analytical method alone. It hopes to point to the false antinomy between revelation and reason, faith and knowledge, grace and nature, courage and anxiety. Mathematics, physics, philosophy, biology, and religion, in spite of their almost complete independence, have begun to sense their interrelatedness and to become aware of that mode of cognition which teaches that "the light is not without but within me, and I myself am the light."

Modern man is threatened by a world created by himself. He is faced with the conversion of mind to naturalism, a dogmatic secularism and an opposition to a belief in the transcendent. He begins to see, however, that the universe is given not as one existing and one perceived but as the unity of subject and object; that the barrier between them cannot be said to have been dissolved as the result of recent experience in the physical sciences, since this barrier has never existed. Confronted with the question of meaning, he is summoned to rediscover and scrutinize the immutable and the permanent which constitute the dynamic, unifying aspect of life as well as the principle of differentiation; to reconcile identity and diversity, immutability and unrest. He begins to recognize that just as every person descends by his particular path, so he is able to ascend, and this ascent aims at a return to the source of creation, an inward home from which he has become estranged.

It is the hope of RELIGIOUS PERSPECTIVES that the rediscovery of man will point the way to the rediscovery of God. To this end a rediscovery of first principles should constitute part of the quest. These principles, not to be superseded by new discoveries, are not those of historical worlds that come to be and perish. They are to be sought in the heart and spirit of man, and no interpretation of a merely historical or scientific universe can guide the search. RELIGIOUS PERSPECTIVES attempts not only to ask dispassionately what the nature of God is, but also to restore to human life at least the hypothesis of God and the symbols that relate to him. It endeavors to show that man is faced with the metaphysical question of the truth of religion while he encounters the empirical question of its effects on the life of humanity and its meaning for society. Religion is here distinguished from theology and its doctrinal forms and is intended to denote the feelings, aspirations, and acts of men, as they relate to total reality. For we are all in search of reality, of a reality which is there whether we know it or not; and the search is of our own making but reality is not.

RELIGIOUS PERSPECTIVES is nourished by the spiritual and intellectual energy of world thought, by those religious and ethical leaders who are not merely spectators but scholars deeply involved in the critical problems common to all religions. These thinkers recognize that human morality and human ideals thrive only when set in a context of a transcendent attitude toward religion and that by pointing to the ground of identity and the common nature of being in the religious experience of man, the essential nature of religion may be defined. Thus, they are committed to reevaluate the meaning of everlastingness, an experience which has been lost and which is the content of that *visio Dei* constituting the structure of all religions. It is the many absorbed everlastingly into the ultimate unity, a unity subsuming what Whitehead calls the fluency of God and the everlastingness of passing experience.

The false dichotomies, created by man, especially by Western man, do not exist in nature. Antinomies are unknown in the realm of nature. The new topology of the earth implies the link between an act and a whole series of consequences; and a consciousness of the individual that every time a decision is made it has distant consequences which become more precisely determined.

Furthermore, man has a desire for "elsewhere," a third dimension which cannot be found on earth and yet which must be experienced on earth: prediction: detailed statement referring to something that is to happen in the future; projection: combining a number of trends; prevision: that which is scientifically probable and likely to happen; prospective: the relation between present activity and the image of the future; plan: the sum of total decisions for coordinated activities with a goal, both spiritual and material, in mind.

The authors in RELIGIOUS PERSPECTIVES attempt to show that to *be* is more important than to have since *being* leads to transcendence and joy, while having alone leads to apathy and despair.

Man has now reached the point of controlling those forces both outside himself and within himself which throughout history hemmed in decision-making. And what is decisive is that this new trend is irreversible. We have eaten of this new tree of knowledge and what fifty years ago seemed *fate* has now become the subject of our deliberate choices. Therefore, for man, both in the East and in the West, the two basic questions are: What proper use can we make of our knowledge both for the spirit and for the body and what are the criteria for our choices? To the correct answers to these questions which conform to the new reality can the continuity of human life be preserved and the human person related not only to the present but also to the past and therefore to the future in a meaningful existence. The choice is ours.

These volumes seek to show that the unity of which we speak consists in a certitude emanating from the nature of man who seeks God and the nature of God who seeks man. Such certitude bathes in an intuitive act of cognition, participating in the divine essence and is related to the natural spirituality of intelligence. This is not by any means to say that there is an equivalence of all faiths in the traditional religions of human history. It is, however, to emphasize the distinction between the spiritual and the temporal which all religions acknowledge. For duration of thought is composed of instants superior to time, and is an intuition of the permanence of existence and its meta-historical reality. In fact, the symbol[1] itself found on cover and jacket of each volume of RELIGIOUS PERSPECTIVES is the visible sign or representation of the essence, immediacy, and timelessness of religious experience; the one immutable center, which may be analogically related to being in pure act, moving with centrifugal and ecumenical necessity outward into the manifold modes, yet simultaneously, with dynamic centripetal power and with full intentional energy, returning to the source. Through the very diversity of its authors, the Series shows that the basic and poignant concern of every faith is to point to, and overcome the crisis in our apocalyptic epoch—the crisis of man's separation from man and of man's separation from God—the failure of love. The authors endeavor, moreover, to illustrate the truth that the human heart is able, and even yearns, to go to the very lengths of God; that the darkness and cold, the frozen spiritual misery of recent times are breaking, cracking, and beginning to move, yielding to efforts to overcome spiritual muteness and moral paralysis. In this way, it is hoped, the immediacy of pain and sorrow, the primacy of tragedy and suffering in human life,

---

[1] From the original design by Leo Katz.

may be transmuted into a spiritual and moral triumph. For the uniqueness of man lies in his capacity for self-transcendence.

RELIGIOUS PERSPECTIVES is therefore an effort to explore the *meaning* of God, an exploration which constitutes an aspect of man's intrinsic nature, part of his ontological substance. This Series grows out of an abiding concern that in spite of the release of man's creative energy which science has in part accomplished, this very science has overturned the essential order of nature. Shrewd as man's calculations have become concerning his means, his choice of ends which was formerly correlated with belief in God, with absolute criteria of conduct, has become witless. God is not to be treated as an exception to metaphysical principles, invoked to prevent their collapse. He is rather their chief exemplification, the sources of all potentiality. The personal reality of freedom and providence, of will and conscience, may demonstrate that "he who knows" commands a depth of consciousness inaccessible to the profane man, and is capable of that transfiguration which prevents the twisting of all good to ignominy. This religious content of experience is not within the province of science to bestow; it corrects the error of treating the scientific account as if it were itself metaphysical or religious; it challenges the tendency to make a religion of science—or a science of religion—a dogmatic act which destroys the moral dynamic of man. Indeed, many men of science are confronted with unexpected implications of their own thought and are beginning to accept, for instance, the trans-spatial and trans-temporal dimension in the nature of reality.

RELIGIOUS PERSPECTIVES attempts to show the fallacy of the apparent irrelevance of God in history. This Series submits that

no convincing image of man can arise, in spite of the many ways
in which human thought has tried to reach it, without a philosophy of human nature and human freedom which does not ex-
clude God. This image of *Homo cum Deo* implies the highest
conceivable freedom, the freedom to step into the very fabric of
the universe, a new formula for man's collaboration with the
creative process and the only one which is able to protect man
from the terror of existence. This image implies further that the
mind and conscience are capable of making genuine discrimina-
tions and thereby may reconcile the serious tensions between the
secular and religious, the profane and sacred. The idea of the
sacred lies in what it *is,* timeless existence. By emphasizing timeless existence against rationalism as a reality, we are liberated, in
our communion with the eternal, from the otherwise unbreak-
able rule of "before and after." Then we are able to admit that
all forms, all symbols in religions, by their negation of error and
their affirmation of the actuality of truth, make it possible to
experience that *knowing* which is above knowledge, and that
dynamic passage of the universe to unending unity.

God is here interpreted not as a heteronomous being issuing
commandments but as the *Tatt-Twam-Asi:* "Do unto others as
you would have others do unto you. For I am the Lord." This
does not mean a commandment from on high but rather a self-
realization through "the other"; since the isolated individual is
unthinkable and meaningless. Man becomes man by recognizing
his true nature as a creature capable of will and decision. For
then the divine and the sacred become manifest. And though he
believes in choices, he is no Utopian expecting the "coming of
the Kingdom." Man, individually and collectively, is losing the
chains which have bound him to the inexorable demands of

nature. The constraints are diminishing and an infinity of choices becomes available to him. Thus man himself, from the sources of his ontological being, at last must decide what is the *bonum et malum*. And though the anonymous forces which in the past have set the constraints do indeed threaten him with total anarchy and with perhaps a worse tyranny than he experienced in past history, he nevertheless begins to see that preceding the moral issue is the cognitive problem: the perception of those conditions for life which permit mankind to fulfill itself and to accept the truth that beyond scientific, discursive knowledge is nondiscursive, intuitive awareness. And, I suggest, this is not to secularize God but rather to gather him into the heart of the nature of matter and indeed of life itself.

The volumes in this Series seek to challenge the crisis which separates, to make reasonable a religion that binds, and to present the numinous reality within the experience of man. Insofar as the Series succeeds in this quest, it will direct mankind toward a reality that is eternal and away from a preoccupation with that which is illusory and ephemeral.

For man is now confronted with his burden and his greatness: "He calleth to me, Watchman, what of the night? Watchman, what of the night?"[2] Perhaps the anguish in the human soul may be assuaged by the answer, by the *assimilation* of the person in God: "The morning cometh, and also the night: if ye will inquire, inquire ye: return, come."[3]

RUTH NANDA ANSHEN

[2] Isaiah 21:11.
[3] Isaiah 21:12.

INTRODUCTION

by Carl Friedrich Freiherr von Weizsäcker

IN EARLY 1968 SOME GERMAN FRIENDS ASKED me to meet Pandit
Gopi Krishna of Srinagar, Kashmir, who at that time was completely unknown to me. I was tempted to make excuses, plead-
ing lack of time. Since my student years I have been fully aware
of the fundamental significance of the Oriental tradition of
meditation and philosophy. I felt close to it but waited a long
time before I studied it seriously. It seemed to me that most of
us, who have been born into Western culture, ought first to

trace the innermost patterns of our culture until our own development itself would lead us into fellowship with Eastern culture.

The current flood of salvation literature, of traveling Yoga masters, and of generally superficial imitations of Eastern practices in Western countries seems to me a rather desperate reaction to the crisis in our own consciousness, a false answer to a valid question.

Fortunately, I did overcome my initial reluctance. When the announced guest entered my room, I felt in the fraction of a second: This man is genuine. He was unassuming and sure of himself, a man who did not show his almost seventy years, who looked his partner firmly in the eyes, was dressed in the native clothing of a Brahman from Kashmir (that light-skinned social class to which Nehru's family also belongs); he answered precise questions precisely, in a sometimes surprising way and with a deeply human sincerity which was often enhanced by a smile. His presence was good for me, and I could feel within me the traces of his simple and good emanations for as long as a month afterwards. I received and read his first book, *Kundalini,* which is the story of his life. From my conversation with him and from the book I learned that he had spent almost his whole life in his native Kashmir. He had been a government official for decades. He is married, his three children are now also married, and to this day he has remained the head of his family in the classical Indian sense. When I recently had the opportunity to visit him for a week in his simple, middle-class home in Srinagar, I saw how much he is an integral part of the society from which he comes. He is a revered leader of the Hindu minority, but he is also respected by the Muslims and has many friends among them. For many years he served as director of a program of assistance for the poor. When one visits a village in his company, many of the peasants recognize him and greet him with enthusiasm. At considerable risk to himself and with great personal courage he has successfully worked for the abolition of outmoded religious customs in his society. Thus he succeeded in changing old ways so that it is now customary to permit widows to remarry, and he has also been instrumental in reducing the intolerable financial burdens connected with the marriage of daughters. It may not be clear to the Western reader how much of a break with tradition this involves. If one knew no more than this, one would say that Gopi Krishna is indeed an outstanding local leader deserving of our respect and affection.

The basic content of my conversation with him and of his book did, however, turn out to be something quite different. It concerns a shattering, life-threatening experience of a this-worldly/other-worldly force which reshapes one's whole personality, the force he calls by its traditional Indian name, *Kundalini*. I am going to discuss the nature of this experience in the third section of this Introduction. Here I am limiting myself to its biographical impact. Gopi Krishna has been meditating since his seventeenth year, at first out of an impulse for personal purification. When he was thirty-four he experienced a breakthrough to a new, enlarged, and blissful consciousness. But the process initiated then resulted in a physical and spiritual transformation which threatened his very existence like an all-consuming fire. He was looking for a master (a guru in the traditional Indian sense) but found no one to help him. Fortu-

3

nately, his ego managed to stay in control of the processes set in motion, which after twelve years resolved themselves into a permanent inner brightness and into a new sense of vitality. He now felt like a new man endowed with objective gifts which he had never had before, such as the gift of inspired writing; he felt like a man who could turn to his fellow men with a new capacity for help and guidance. He actively discouraged a rapidly spreading movement in his native region to establish him as a famous enlightened one, since he was critical of this kind of fervor; his way of dealing with his fellow men lay in the realm of controllable reality. Yet he was sure that he had experienced the awakening of *Kundalini* described in classical literature. He studied the writings of the meditative and mystic traditions as one who understood their meaning. After he had spent decades in self-examination he decided to write about his experiences for the world, particularly the world of modern science. His first book was a description of his personal experience. The second book, which is being presented here in RELIGIOUS PERSPECTIVES, constitutes an introduction to the objective lessons he plans to teach in future works.

I myself am writing an Introduction to this book because I would like to contribute to its understanding and its effect. To do so it is necessary that I also point out its weaknesses. Those of us who read this book as modern intellectuals note a certain naivete on the part of the author. He is a mixture of a wholly traditional and a wholly modern man. His values, particularly the moral values of the tradition in which he grew up, are self-evident for him. He is incapable of even a trace of that cynicism with which every, even the most sincere, modern intellectual has been inoculated and which has infected the whole world of contemporary thinking. We intellectuals naively assume that those who lack this inoculation are living in ignorance of something decisively important. That may well be, but in this instance we shall have to move away from our own naïveté in order to comprehend the potential insights of another kind of naivete. On the other hand, Gopi Krishna is quite modern in the sense that he deliberately addresses himself to the modern consciousness, particularly to modern science. He is far removed from Hindu orthodoxy, and I have seen him get into irresolvable differences of opinion with Europeans who tried to play the Indian tradition against that of the modern West. The problem arising here is that his knowledge of European intellectual concepts and of modern science is autodidactic. He does not always clearly distinguish between the customary academic classification of a scientific doctrine and its more subtle meanings. He is therefore not always a competent analyst, but he is something far more important: he is an eyewitness to the truth he represents. Even his sometimes broadly flowing stream of words, a style not unusual in India, is indicative of the way he composes his writings which are not the result of reflection but flow from the compelling force of a spontaneous, self-repeating awareness.

2. *Religion as a Problem and Science as a Problem*

The two introductory chapters of Gopi Krishna's book merely raise questions on which the answers beginning in the third chapter are based.

The first chapter considers religion as a problem. It starts out like an Enlightenment critique of religion, noting the irrationality and the repulsive practices from shamanism to the more advanced forms of religion. It then deals with the unsolved problem of theodicy, the justification of God against the charges arising from the sufferings of the creature, and discusses at some length the frequently contradictory doctrines of immortality in the many religions. It compares the contradictions among doctrines of revelation with the sure certainty of science and predicts the inevitable demise of the dominion of religion over man. In view of the unbroken religiosity of most Hindus this prediction is more radical than it sounds in the Western Christian world where in fact this has already largely come about.

But Gopi Krishna has no intention to advocate an anti-religious enlightenment philosophy here; he intends rather to formulate a paradox. If religion is so full of contradictions, how could it have been a guide to mankind for thousands of years? He confronts the opponents of religion, who consider themselves enlightened, with an unresolved problem. Perhaps we can explain this with the conceptual model of dialectics which —thanks to Neo-Marxism—has again become popular among Western young people. Dialectical philosophy of history considers the dominion of religion as a phase of world history which today has already been overcome as a matter of fact. The dialectic of history, however, implies that there is truth in each phase of history. But the truth of each phase is driven beyond itself to its explicit negation by its inherent contradictions. If for the sake of simplicity we argue that the historical era of religion has been overcome by the scientific era, it follows that science itself will remain caught in an attitude of naïve opposition to religion until it can ask to what extent there has been truth in the very religion it has replaced. This question must be asked unflinchingly and in view of the contradictions and the horror of religion, or it is not a question about the reality of religion.

In Gopi Krishna's second chapter it appears that science, which dominates our world, has not been able to ask this question because it has just experienced the collapse of the very world it has created and ruled. This opinion may be divided: During the epoch of its unbroken predominance natural science —and that is what we are talking about—has been unable even to pose the question of the truth of religion. It has been naïvely materialistic and has simply denied existing realities which did not fit into its concepts. (This indicates, by the way, what kind of writings Gopi Krishna read in his youth. I remember how I struggled with the popular philosophy of the natural sciences in my student days. But at the university I was fortunate enough to be able to study Bohr's and Heisenberg's physics as well as classical European philosophy.) Today the whole modern world reveals the crisis brought about by living in a society which is determined by scientific concepts. Gopi Krishna sees this crisis manifested particularly in the breakdown of moral values which at one time had been protected by religion. His views may not seem to convince the social critics among the younger generation who have their own form of moral protest. Yet even their criticism may be seen as pointing in the direction Gopi Krishna has indicated.

The younger generation is engaged in an attack against what may be called technocracy. In the West, technocracy appears primarily in the form of capitalism, in the East as bureaucracy. These two terms imply the rather obvious charge that the owners of private capital or the functionaries of a party apparatus are placing their personal interest above that of society as a whole. This charge may be more thoroughly justified if we first consider seriously the plea entered by both capitalists and bureaucrats that they are playing an indispensable role in their respective social systems. On the surface, however, the political struggle today is waged by ideologists. As a matter of principle the ideologists consider one of the two systems as essentially wrong and the other as right with the proviso that their respective system, the right one, has admittedly and regrettably not yet reached its final and perfect form. I am willing to leave this contest to those who believe in it; I am just asking the liberals and the socialists why capital and why the apparatus of party and state have failed so miserably. For that is the point at which the charges against technocracy acquire their proper dimension. In both instances the purveyors of the means, the masters of technology, have declared their independence and are no longer serving the whole of society. But as long as these charges remain matters of individual morality, they share the weakness of any mere moralizing. They must address themselves to the basis of the problem and inquire what it is in these systems that results in an almost irresistible temptation for the means to become independent of the ends.

As a possible answer I submit that the reason may be found in the very technological nature of both of these social systems, in the conceptual and operational separation of means from ends which is inherent in them. In his book *Physics and Beyond; Encounters and Conversations,** Heisenberg says that as a matter

* Vol. 42 in WORLD PERSPECTIVES, planned and edited by Ruth Nanda Anshen.

of principle, political systems have to be judged by their means and not by their ends. Gandhi taught a way of political struggle which ruled out any means not in keeping with the desired goal; he believed that a nonviolent state can be reached only by nonviolent means. But the linear-causal manner of technological thinking sharply distinguishes between ends and means. It considers this distinction to be justified by the classical natural sciences. I am reminded here of a remark my uncle Victor von Weizsäcker once made to me, "All three, capitalism, state socialism, and modern physics, are forms of the same mistake." (In the context given at the time, he did not speak of state socialism.) This brings us back to Gopi Krishna's chapter heading, "The Error of Science." The dissolution of reality into a network of causal chains is a mistake. A culture which misunderstands reality that way destroys the very reality it intends to control and improve.

To use the dialectical pattern of thinking again, there is also truth in science. Reality may be rendered objective by reducing it to a network of causes. This enterprise has been highly successful. But what has been lost in the process? At this point the question of the truth of religion ought to arise.

If we inquire, with the scientist's openness to any kind of experience, about the truth which might have been concealed in religion, it may be that we find the juxtaposition of dogmatic religion and dogmatic science "suspended" by a new truth. I use the term "suspended" in the dual sense in which Hegel also used it, that is, as overcome and at the same time preserved in what essentially constitutes its truth. To be sure, this kind of truth probably will no longer require the dialectical pattern of thinking, which has as its main spring conceptual, hence objectivizing reflection upon the results of objectivizing.

Gopi Krishna's thought and language are much simpler and more direct. He sees the ancient religious writings permeated by hints of a spiritual law. To discover that law he set out on his quest long ago. His contributions to the problem today are not just vague speculations but above all accounts of his own personal experience. His first two chapters give the personal background of this personal experience. According to his autobiography *Kundalini*, it was precisely the insufficiency of religion and science which agitated him in his younger years. It caused him to search for an inner opening towards a higher, spiritual reality by constant meditation which he repeated daily before sunrise each morning.

3. *The Experience of Gopi Krishna*

"One morning during the Christmas of 1937 I sat cross-legged in a small room in a little house on the outskirts of the town of Jammu, the winter capital of the Jammu and Kashmir State in northern India. I was meditating with my face towards the window on the east through which the first grey streaks of the slowly brightening dawn fell into the room. Long practice had accustomed me to sit in the same posture for hours at a time without the least discomfort, and I sat breathing slowly and rhythmically, my attention drawn towards the crown of my head, contemplating an imaginary lotus in full bloom, radiating light.

"I sat steadily, unmoving and erect, my thoughts uninterruptedly centered on the shining lotus, intent on keeping my attention from wandering and bringing it back again and again whenever it moved in any other direction. The intensity of concentration interrupted my breathing; gradually it slowed down to such an extent that at times it was barely perceptible. My whole being was so engrossed in the contemplation of the lotus that for several minutes at a time I lost touch with my body and surroundings. During such intervals I used to feel as if I were poised in mid-air, without any feeling of a body around me. The only object of which I was aware was a lotus of brilliant colour, emitting rays of light. This experience has happened to many people who practise meditation in any form regularly for a sufficient length of time, but what followed on that fateful morning in my case, changing the whole course of my life and outlook, has happened to few.

"During one such spell of intense concentration I suddenly felt a strange sensation below the base of my spine, at the place touching the seat, while I sat cross-legged on a folded blanket spread on the floor. The sensation was so extraordinary and so pleasing that my attention was forcibly drawn towards it. The moment my attention was thus unexpectedly withdrawn from the point on which it was focused, the sensation ceased. Thinking it to be a trick played by my imagination to relax the tension, I dismissed the matter from my mind and brought my attention back to the point from which it had wandered. Again I fixed it on the lotus, and as the image grew clear and distinct at the top of my head, again the sensation occurred. This time I tried to maintain the fixity of my attention and succeeded for a few seconds, but the sensation extending upwards grew so intense and was so extraordinary, as compared to anything I had experienced before, that in spite of myself my mind went towards it, and at that very moment it again disappeared. I was now convinced that something unusual had happened for which my daily practice of concentration was probably responsible.

"I had read glowing accounts, written by learned men, of great benefits resulting from concentration, and of the miraculous powers acquired by yogis through such exercises. My heart began to beat wildly, and I found it difficult to bring my attention to the required degree of fixity. After a while I grew composed and was soon as deep in meditation as before. When completely immersed I again experienced the sensation, but this time, instead of allowing my mind to leave the point where I had fixed it, I maintained a rigidity of attention throughout. The sensation again extended upwards, growing in intensity, and I felt myself wavering; but with a great effort I kept my attention centered on the lotus. Suddenly, with a roar like that of a waterfall, I felt a stream of liquid light entering my brain through the spinal cord.

Entirely unprepared for such a development, I was completely taken by surprise; but regaining self-control instantaneously, I remained sitting in the same posture, keeping my mind on the point of concentration. The illumination grew brighter and brighter, the roaring louder, I experienced a rocking sensation and then felt myself slipping out of my body, entirely enveloped in a halo of light. It is impossible to describe the experience accurately. I felt the point of consciousness that was myself growing wider, surrounded by waves of light. It grew wider and wider, spreading outward while the body, normally the immediate object of its perception, appeared to have receded into the distance until I became entirely unconscious of it. I was now all consciousness, without any outline, without any idea of a corporeal appendage, without any feeling or sensation coming from the senses, immersed in a sea of light simultaneously conscious and aware of every point, spread out, as it were, in all directions without any barrier or material obstruction. I was no longer myself, or to be more accurate, no longer as I knew myself to be, a small point of awareness confined in a body, but instead was a vast circle of consciousness in which the body was but a point, bathed in light and in a state of exaltation and happiness impossible to describe.

"After some time, the duration of which I could not judge, the circle began to narrow down; I felt myself contracting, becoming smaller and smaller, until I again became dimly conscious of the outline of my body, then more clearly; and as I slipped back to my old condition, I became suddenly aware of the noises in the street, felt again my arms and legs and head, and once more became my narrow self in touch with my body and surroundings. When I opened my eyes and looked about, I felt a little dazed and bewildered, as if coming back from a strange land completely foreign to me. The sun had risen and was shining full on my face, warm and soothing. I tried to lift my hands, which always rested in my lap, one upon the other, during meditation. My arms felt limp and lifeless. With an effort I raised them up and stretched them to enable the blood to flow freely. Then I tried to free my legs from the posture in which I was sitting and to place them in a more comfortable position but could not. They were heavy and stiff. With the help of my hands I freed them and stretched them out, then leaned back against the wall, reclining in a position of ease and comfort."*

This report is the beginning of Krishna's book *Kundalini*. I thought it imperative to cite it verbatim. At the risk of belaboring the self-evident I would like to draw the reader's attention to a few notable features of this report.

First, there is the accuracy of self-observation, especially the description of physical phenomena. The another retains his orientation and communicates it to the reader. Year and season, place and hour of the day, bodily posture and state of consciousness are duly noted. The physiological location of the phenomenon is the central nervous system: spine and brain. The sensation originates at the base of the spine, as the result of concentration, moves upward, and penetrates the brain like a roaring stream of light. Now consciousness expands spatially and becomes much larger than the body, corporeality disappears, and there is an experience of light and unspeakable bliss. Time also has vanished—"how long it had lasted, I couldn't say"—and after awhile the circle contracts again, consciousness again becomes aware of its limits, he opens his eyes; the whole experience has taken but a fraction of the time from dawn to sunrise, a space of time particularly short in the tropics. Laboriously he regains mastery of his limbs, arms, and legs; he leans his back against the wall, relaxed.

Further on in the text there is a sketch of the objective prerequisites for this experience: seventeen years of practice in meditation; the objective symbol of divine consciousness in the

---

* *Kundalini* by Gopi Krishna, pp. 11-13. Revised edition © copyright 1970 in Great Britain by Vincent Stuart & John M. Watkins Ltd., London. Used by permission of Robinson & Watkins.

image of the thousand-leaf lotus crowning the head; the ancient tradition that the "serpentine force" of Kundalini rests at the base of the spine coiled into three and a half windings and that if it is awakened it transforms consciousness. Against this background it is worth noting that in Gopi Krishna's report there is a threefold interplay of question and answer between human consciousness, the unmoved lotus, and the awakening serpent. Consciousness concentrates on nothing but the lotus. It required seventeen years to purify and fortify one's concentration to the point where the serpent stirs from its slumber. The bliss of its awakening, experienced in the form of physical sensation, distracts consciousness from the lotus and behold, the serpent recoils and the experience vanishes. Not on itself does the serpent want to focus attention, but only on the lotus blossom. When consciousness finally manages this, the serpent rises up to the lotus like a torrent moving through the seat of consciousness. If, as a hint for Western readers, I may be permitted for a moment to substitute our metaphysical terms God, man, and nature—which have lost so much of their meaning for us—for the terms lotus, consciousness, and serpent, then we would have to spell out Gopi Krishna's experience as follows: Nature seeks unity with God through man and in the particular man who does not look towards her but only towards God. The man who opens up that path for her is blessed by nature with the torrent of her bliss, with the realization of a new sphere of consciousness.*

* Here it must be noted that according to the conventional tradition of Kundalini Yoga the serpentine power may also be raised to the level of lower centers, hence to lower goals, as for example to the mere purpose of revitalizing the sexual or vital potency of a person. Gopi Krishna himself explains the worldly genius of the artist and the scientist as a raising of Kundalini to the second-highest center. According to tradition, however, only a raising of the power to the highest center leads to the mystic consciousness.

Obviously, Gopi Krishna did not reflect on all this at that moment, rather he experienced it as an unexplained fact.

Anyone who thinks that the experience opened up a path to happiness for the author has failed to note carefully certain hints already contained in the account we have cited above. After the experience, the authors limbs were stiff and useless. The book goes on to tell how the following day was spent in restlessness and exhaustion, how sleep refused to come in the subsequent night, and how a weakened repetition of the experience the next morning left the author in an even greater state of exhaustion. After a few days he lost his power of concentration and with it also any renewed experience of bliss and his previous capacity for living a well-ordered everyday life. What did remain was an ever-growing inner stream of fire in every nerve, sexual excitement, thundering sounds, a maelstrom of copper-colored lights wildly rushing into each other, an unbearable, dry, burning inner brightness by day and night. To his horror he was losing even the most elementary feelings of human contact, his love for his wife and children. The account of this development in the book appears to be supported by the fact that it lacks the definite structure of the portion cited earlier. Rather, it describes in trying, confusing, repetitious language the deadly, torturous sensations and struggles which the conscious personality of the author carried on against this maelstrom for two months with unbelievable outward discipline but with a feeling of ebbing strength. (He told only *one* person what was going on within him.)

He tried to understand what was happening to him with every intellectual means at his disposal. In the Yoga literature available to him he found a description of the awakening of Kundalini. In spite of constant doubts he came to recognize his own experience with growing certainty. But the literature, which praised this phenomenon as the gift of a higher power, barely hinted at the dangers involved. It told of three channels through which the power can rise: the central one, called *Susumna*, which is the one properly intended for it, and two side channels, which Gopi Krishna now identifies with the sympathetic and parasympathetic nervous systems. *Pingala*, the right side channel, is linked with the sun, with heat and excitement. *Ida*, the left one, represents the moon, coolness and restraint. If the power rises up in one of the side channels only, it can be deadly because of "heat" or "cold." In his youth, Gopi Krishna now says, the hot side of his physical make-up had been strongly overactive while the cool side had been underactive. In his extreme need, which seemed to have insanity as the only possible outcome, it occurred to him that the power might have risen within him only by way of the hot channel. With all his remaining strength of consciousness he therefore concentrated on the left, the cool side. "Then, as if it had been waiting for this fateful moment, a miracle occurred. There was a sound, as if a nerve were tearing. Suddenly, a silver vein ran crisscross through my spine just like the slithering motions of a white serpent in quick flight which brought a brilliant, cascading shower of radiant vital force into my brain." He had been saved; sleep was returning to him and he slowly recovered.

I am omitting Gopi Krishna's lengthy description of the next twelve years which is permeated with many theoretical considerations. The energy within him, his physical and psychic transformation continued while outwardly he was leading a normal, though vulnerable and somewhat restricted life. Human warmth and devotion to duty returned. His closeness to his wife, who devotedly cared for him, saved him in recurring crises. Yet ten years later, when his daughter was married, he still was unable to turn to his family with any sort of overt closeness, as his son-in-law has told me. A number of positive changes did eventually take place. The inward experience of brightness, for example, was transformed into a constant awareness of all the colors of the external world with new, definite radiance. But an attempt to return to meditation ended in renewed and deeper disaster after a brief moment of joyous possession. Gopi Krishna was unable to find a master anywhere who could guide him. His spirit became agitated by the question whether the change in his inner awareness, which was of no use to his fellow men, had really been worth the lifelong effort it had cost him or whether it had actually spoiled all meaningful living for him. The English edition of *Kundalini* includes a running commentary by J. Hillman, who carefully traces this whole development in terms of Jungian psychology. Gopi Krishna's own interpretation is outlined in his two books.

Early in 1950 Gopi Krishna experienced a final transition to a stable consciousness, open to, yet not dependent on, the outside world. The transition occurred in connection with his inspired writing. He had completely abandoned his active meditating, but he would occasionally and without effort permit himself to be submerged into the ocean of consciousness surrounding him. He had never had any interest in poetry. Now he was feeling a desire for poetry. He recited to himself mystical verse he liked, attempted to write, and one day at the center of a bridge in the middle of a crowd of people there flowed "past my eyes like radiant writing in the air, which vanished as fast as it had come, . . . two lines of a marvelous poem in Kashmiri . . . like a mighty presence rising from nowhere, embracing me and overshadowing all objects around me." On that same day Gopi Krishna entered a cosmic consciousness that turned whatever he had experienced as explosive and fiery twelve years ago into definite reality which was "like an ocean of life moving from within" (p. 172). I am not going to reproduce the account of this awareness here. I shall return to it later, for this transcends the biographical and properly belongs to the subject itself. But this is the experience which induced Gopi Krishna to write poetry.

The first lines that came to him were a continuation of the couplet which had appeared before his eyes on the bridge. Then he wrote additional Kashmiri poems. A few days later poems appeared in Urdu, then in Panjabi. Gopi Krishna knew all these languages. "But my astonishment knew no bounds, when a few days later I received instructions to prepare myself to receive verses in Persian. I had never read the language nor could I speak it. I was waiting in breathless excitement and immediately following this forewarning several Persian verses flashed through my brain. . . . Since the language of Kashmiri is rich in Persian words, I found it easy to understand those which were current in my native language. After I had exerted a sufficient measure of concentration and effort I finally succeeded in writing down these lines. But there were many blank spaces, which I was only able to fill in and correct much later" (p. 176). Next there followed a poem in the German language, a language which even today is completely unknown to him consciously, a French and an Italian poem, and finally a few lines in Sanskrit.

I can feel the inevitably growing annoyance of my scientifically trained readers, for I felt the same way when I read this account. One is inclined to read this story as the twelve-year history of an identity crisis of a sensitive personality, which borders the psychotic. At the same time one must admit that a man who has lived through such a crisis knows a few things which may be of importance to the rest of us. But why does this story have to end in miracles? Would anything be lacking in a mature and inspired personality if he were to write poems in just those languages he has learned? It is difficult for me to overcome my scientific skepticism which has been schooled in the psychology of reliable witnesses. I openly admit that reading this particular section of the book I felt for the first time: "Here the imaginative memory is running away with the author; I'd like to see the German poem before I believe it."

But I must honor the facts. Since then I have seen the poem, for it was published privately in 1952. The German poem is everything but a perfect dictation of a—by human standards— perfect intelligence. It is, if one may say so, touching. The poem is written in erratic German, scarcely adequate in expression, reminiscent of a folk song, a naïve communication of an unquestionable experience. In view of the cynicism of intellectual critics I don't feel justified in reproducing the whole poem. A few lines out of context may serve as an example:

> Ein schöner Vogel immer singt
> In meinem Herz mit leisem Ton . . .
> Und wenn vergiest der Nachtwind auf

> Die grünen Gräser seine Tränen, . . .
> Dann der Vogel wacht.*

Just as the German poem is German in the way of a German folksong, so the Italian poem is written like an Italian folksong: it rhymes *cuore* with *amore*. Although the rhyme patterns are naïve, the English poem expresses moral imperatives to the nations of the world in a voice of great prophecy.

> O people of the world unite
>   And pave the way to peace sublime;
> Divided you yourself invite
>   Disastrous wars, unrest and crime.

What makes this poetic phenomenon possible and what purpose does it serve? I do not know. Honor the incomprehensible!

What followed next in Gopi Krishna's life was the period of intense, sensitive, and wise service to society I mentioned in the first section of this Introduction, a demonstration of restored health and clear thinking. After this period he also studied traditional Yoga in search of an explanation of what he was certain he had experienced. In his seventieth year Gopi Krishna tried to draw the attention of Western science, particularly of medicine, to the phenomena he had experienced in order to point out their significance. This period is also the point of departure for a later, formally much better, prophetic poem in English describing the horrors of a war which he believes the current

---

* A beautiful bird always sings
  In my heart with a soft voice . . .
  And when the nightwind sheds
  Its tears on the green grass, . . .
  Then the bird is watching.

course of mankind will inevitably bring about. According to Gopi Krishna's interpretation, the poem is not intended as an actual prophecy which reads the future as if it had already happened, but it predicts the inescapable consequences of what is happening today. We talked about this at my first meeting with him. At that time he said simply: "The nations of the earth will be united. But war is inevitable." He meant a world war. He expressed what I had been feeling for a long time but had not dared to think about clearly. Indeed, we cannot escape thinking of it that way: "War is inevitable unless what is necessary happens." But what is necessary?

In view of the importance of this question we can understand Gopi Krishna's urgent desire to share with the world that which he has experienced as necessary. The story of his life is more than the history of a pathological disturbance with a happy end only if it provides us with empirical data to understand an objective situation. This objective element is more than a simple moral appeal which we already know to be ineffective. The question is, Why do people act morally or immorally? In Gopi Krishna's view, the point at issue is a spiritual law. What is unique about his view is that this spiritual law is at the same time a biological law. That is why it must be tested in terms of a mode of questioning proper to our natural sciences. He is anxious to have each one of his assertions tested by independent authorities. He is particularly interested in an empirical test. Those who know Western science are aware that it tends to confront almost exclusively only those problems for which it is theoretically prepared, at least in terms of the conceptual framework of the problem. What follows is intended to assist in such a preparation.

4. *The Biological-Medical Aspect*

Gopi Krishna's biological view may be briefly summed up conceptually. The spiritual law is by its very nature biological law as well. It is the law of evolution. Although to my knowledge Krishna does not explicitly say so anywhere, he does imply that the lower is designed to develop into the higher and that in fact it does so develop. To conceptualize this process of evolution he uses two concepts taken from traditional Indian thought: *Prana* and *Kundalini.*

Prana is the all-penetrating, subtle life substance. *Prana* is material, composed of exceedingly fine stuff, as it is occasionally described. Gopi Krishna considers the materiality of *Prana* very important and likes to support this in conversation by citing the well-known line from the *Upanishads:* "*Prana* comes from nutrition." But at the same time *Prana* appears as a substance belonging to the soul; according to Gopi Krishna *Prana* is the food of developing human consciousness. Finally, *Prana* is something like the omnipresent energy of the highest cosmic intelligence. *Prana* meaningfully builds all of life according to a plan which is hidden from us, yet partially disclosed to a searching view.

The Western scientist faced with such concepts is apt to admit his confusion which—as long as he is sure of his own conceptual basis—he will casually blame "those prescientific Hindu views." Our natural sciences today, particularly biology and medicine, are based on a strictly Cartesian separation of matter from consciousness. As long as we believe in the methodological necessity of this separation we are bound to argue, "If *Prana* claims to be matter, then we have to keep it strictly separate from such concepts as consciousness; otherwise

Prana would belong to the realm of psychology and has nothing to do with physics." Now this point of view is a relic of a way of thinking, which in its basic conception is considered to be highly fragile even by many of those who cannot find anything better to take its place. Since the formulation of quantum theory, physics no longer holds this point of view but it has obvious problems in formulating a better one. The cybernetic attempt to simulate psychic phenomena with the help of material models is based on a belief in unity which is difficult to articulate. In the last analysis, I do not consider it detrimental that in the practice of behavioral research we do in fact hardly ever succeed in sticking to purely behavioral language and to avoid all "subjective" or "anthropomorphic" expressions. It seems to me that at this point practice is smarter than the theory by which it explains itself.

The evolutionary potency is called *Kundalini*. It is closely linked with sexual potency as indicated by the location of the "serpent" in close proximity to the sex organs. The evolutionary force functions in two separate stages. In animals it functions directly by way of sexual reproduction. In their case the more highly developed are physical descendants of the less developed. In the case of man there is a development of consciousness, which newly builds up in each individual on the basis of his physical equipment, especially the central nervous system. This evolution of consciousness has its own two stages. Today all men have normal self-consciousness in common, but Gopi Krishna takes a hypothetical look at prehistoric times, when our normal consciousness may have been manifest in the higher anthropoids only sporadically and as a deviation from the then normal state. The higher stage of consciousness even to this day manifests itself only in ingenious and mystically gifted individual persons who often feel as lost and homeless among their own fellow beings and in their everyday consciousness shaped by ideas based on societal norms as H. C. Andersen's "ugly duckling." It is Gopi Krishna's thesis that the development of consciousness is also nurtured by the sexual powers contained in *Kundalini*. On pages 34 to 39 of the present work he describes how, in his own personal experience, the substance of his seed or its *Prana* penetrates the nervous system and nourishes the nerves which are becoming the instruments of higher consciousness.

The modern scientist is again going to hold his breath at this description and ask himself whether he should continue to follow the argument. Let us try to break down the problem.

It has been a thesis of European science since the nineteenth century that the development of animals occurs through lines of physical descent, a thesis which Gopi Krishna as well as other evolutionist Indian thinkers (especially Shri Aurobindo) simply have adopted. But the notion that there is a special "force of evolution" contradicts a dominant doctrine in contemporary biology, the Darwinian theory of natural selection. This conceals a very subtle theoretical problem which I shall consider in section 6. For now, the modern biologist may acclimate himself to Gopi Krishna's manner of speaking by a change in terminology. The material substructure of development in contemporary genetics is chromosomes. These are passed on from generation to generation through the reproductive cells. In that sense animals have the material "force of evolution" located in their sex organs.

We do not feel that there is a conceptual problem in the assertion that man, quite apart from possible further biological evolution, has consciousness as the basis of his development. It is "the nature of man to have history." Due to the influence of sociological thinking we see this development above all in the transformation and renewal of cultural traditions transmitted by society. Both sides agree that there is such a social development. But Gopi Krishna's interest does not lie in the social interactions through which this development takes place. In a way which may just as well be called personal as biological, he is interested in individual consciousness as the carrier of this development. Here he does depart from the doctrine prevailing in the modern sociologized West in two ways, mildly in one instance and sharply in the other. The milder departure is in keeping with our classical historiography. He stresses more emphatically than we do at present the historical role of outstanding personalities without, however, isolating them from the social process. This almost certainly reflects, at least in part, the bias of the historiography which influenced him in his youth. But mature judgment will admit that this is no more than a question of differing nuances. Who can deny the force exerted on the course of history by such diverse personalities as Gandhi and Hitler in this century alone or question the influence of men like Kant and Marx, Plato and Shankara, Christ and Buddha, on the thoughts and actions of men in past centuries?

The other theme is a sharper departure from our way of thinking. At the center of his entire argument Krishna places an evolution of the organ of consciousness which can be described in physiological terms. Our sciences know nothing whatever of such an evolution. This is the field of contest: We enter the fray with a preliminary skirmish by emphasizing first a number of parallels which can be assimilated to our way of thinking and may even be surprisingly similar. Considered from a purely psychological point of view (something Gopi Krishna, of course, does not do), his thesis of the fundamental importance of sexuality in the formation of consciousness directly reminds us of Freudian teaching. Where Gopi Krishna speaks of an elevation of the seminal fluid in language which must seem purely symbolic to the psychologist, Freud speaks of the sublimation of the libido. The latter is more abstract and somewhat obscures the fact that these are essentially the same concepts. Freud treats libido like a substance to which a principle of conservation may be applied; and what does sublimate mean, if not elevate or rise up? More interesting than this rough parallel, however, is the difference between the two views. For Gopi Krishna evolution is essentially determined by its goal. For him sexual potency is the "nourishment" of a higher structure. Freud, on the other hand, represents a form of psychological reductionism. The culture he loves and defends is for him "really" sublimated libido, just as for the classical atomist a crystal is "really" a mass of atoms arranged in a pattern and for the biological physicalist a bird of paradise is "really" an orderly system of organic molecules.

I do believe that it is quite difficult to articulate this contrast clearly and that it may possibly disappear altogether on precise reflection. But the trouble with the contending representatives of both points of view is exactly that they fail to engage in such precise reflection. In Freud the failure has as its consequence that his reductionist theory fails to attain the conceptual level required to interpret his own practice. The psychoanalytic healing of a neurosis is based on the idea that the patient recognizes the forces which beset him as his own actions and that he acknowledges them as his own. He has to recognize himself in his subconscious. As long as he is saying, "They have done this to me" or "That's the way one's drives are," he cannot be healed. He must recognize: "I wanted this myself"; "This is I." One might say, healing occurs only through truth. But *I* and *truth* are "higher" concepts than *sexuality* or *libido*. Formally, "higher" can mean only bringing together a greater complexity in unity. The reduction of the higher to the lower becomes dangerous at the point where it keeps us from using concepts proper for the higher unity. To this I shall also return in section 6. Even though Gopi Krishna's finalistic way of thinking is still quite obscure from the standpoint of the natural sciences, it does at any rate avoid that kind of danger.

Freud's thesis of sexuality has by now lost some of its influence even in psychoanalysis. Also, some of the details of Gopi Krishna's thought remind us of the later teachings of Wilhelm Reich, which do, however, seem to be inferior to the Indian tradition as interpreted by Gopi Krishna. Still, all these comparisons obscure the fundamental difference. Gopi Krishna presents the sexual substance as *nourishment* of consciousness and not as its *essence*. His image of these phenomena is physiological and makes the claim of openness to physiological examination. It is a constantly recurring thought in his writings that no natural scientist will doubt the reality of these phenomena once he has observed and measured them.

But does not the conflict here become finally inevitable and irreconcilable? What can physiology make of the thesis that the seminal substance wanders along the nerve paths to the brain?

And how are we to account for the physiological difference between male and female sexuality here? The problem gets even worse for the Western scientist when he becomes aware of the close relationship of these ideas to the popular notion in India that sexual abstinence is valuable so that as many seeds as possible may be stored in the brain and serve as its source of strength. To this our author replies that it is not the seeds which stream forth but the *Prana* which is produced together with them.

This answer evades the field of conflict but it also removes the problem from the arena where it is open for testing. Reproductive cells can be observed, but we can be a priori certain that they are not to be found in the nerve paths. The natural scientist has absolutely no idea of what *Prana* is; how could he measure it? Yet it is the honest intent of the author to encourage an empirical test precisely at this point. He has made a large number of somatic observations on himself which I did not mention in the previous section. These, above all, are in the realm of bodily sensations which in Yoga are always carefully observed and classified. Here he feels constantly constrained to use terms analogous to physics such as "current," "radiation," etc. His observations also refer to the great importance of the exact dosage of food intake. I believe that a physician might find them of interest and that it should be possible to construct a "dictionary" translating physical sensations into physiological concepts. This may at least become a prolegomenon to a physiological classification of *Prana*.

Another preliminary remark about the basic principle of the *Prana* concept may be in order. In our view the nerves transport information and not a substance. It is necessary, therefore, to ask how *Prana* relates to our concept of information. I shall return to this question in section 7.

I conclude this section with a remark about the significance of sexual potency and sexual abstinence. Because of the distances between the operations of the various sciences, certain obvious questions are being asked too infrequently. The European scholars of history have generally informed themselves and us insufficiently about the significance of sexuality for culture. Even where they considered themselves enlightened, they naïvely continued the repression of sexuality they inherited from the Christian culture where it originated. (As a philosophy instructor, I was able to observe, for example, a certain embarrassment with this kind of subject in the interpretation of Plato's *Symposium*.) The counterattack of psychoanalysis, of the novelist and of the subculture of the modern intellectual (not to speak of the modern sex industry) accepts a different presupposition without questioning: the omnipresence of the sexual drive. Here we can learn from evolutionist biology. Constant readiness for sexual intercourse is, biologically speaking, a peculiarity of the primates, if not of man alone. It is precisely not the "animal in man" which looks for constant sexual fulfillment. It is much easier to convince a deer than a human of the morality of limiting sex to procreation; moreover, the deer has no need for moral injunctions. I have felt for a long time that it is a profound and puzzling problem, worthy of considerable reflection, that pansexuality, war, religion, and science are specifically human traits. Only when this is understood can we comprehend the cultural role of the suppression of sexuality and with it the premisses of our compartmentalization of the sciences into those dealing with the "mind" and those dealing with the "body."

Gopi Krishna tackles this problem in the uninhibited manner of a self-taught man (p. 38). For him unlimited sexual potency in man has the purpose of creating a reservoir for the nourishment of evolution. He regards the suppression of sexuality out of hatred and contempt for the "lower nature" a misunderstanding. It could occur only in the late phase of religious development when the purely biological meaning of sexual abstinence was no longer understood. As a matter of fact, an explanation of sexual repression as contempt for nature fails to make clear where the impulse for this contempt originates in the first place. The Hindu (but not only the Hindu) thesis of Gopi Krishna does make this clear. At issue is not a choice between good and evil but between good and better. Sexuality may serve evolution in reproduction or in the heightening of consciousness. But at certain stages of intensity in the development of consciousness it is insufficient for both purposes in most men who experience this at all. That is why the meaningful ideal of continence has come about, but—to express it in Catholic-Christian terminology—it arises as "evangelical council" for those who can use this advice and not as a commandment for all.

These thoughts were not new to me when I met Gopi Krishna. He merely placed them into context within an over-all point of view. I feel that, at the very least, this way of putting the question is the only way which promises a solution of the riddle of human sexuality and of its role in culture.

5. *Genius and Insanity*

Gopi Krishna talks about the biological basis of religion and genius, which is the area where his thought may find its principal application. He sees religion primarily in the figure of the religious genius. His theme is not everyday religion but the founder of religion, who has brought about everyday religion in the first place, and the mystic who has left it behind. Even negative manifestations of creativity are included. In tyrants, the great destroyers and evil men of world history, he sees *Kundalini* at work. He reminds us of the dual figure of the great goddess *Durga* and *Kali;* it is Kali who dances on the corpse of her husband. He also finds negative manifestations of creativity in those who have lost their normal footing, the insane and those who move at the edge of insanity.

Given his point of departure his choice is perfectly clear. His own experience had been completely extraordinary; it was his singular personal achievement in spite of this to continue within the frame of normal everyday living. The lives of extraordinary figures resonate, therefore, in the strings of his own experience, and he has a sense for the qualitative difference between an extraordinary human experience and all other experiences. The acknowledgment of this difference has nothing to do with the recognition that all men are equal before God, before the law, and in the need to love their neighbor. But they are also equal in that each is unmistakably this one and none other. It is not love for one's neighbor but hatred to deny him the right of being a unique individual. The creativity described by the author is not a claim but a destiny, hence a challenge. An "evil genius" is most often precisely the man who reflects his power and honor on his own ego, power and honor which properly belong only to the force giving him life. For the "good man," far beyond ambition, there lies in wait the temptation of pride.

It will also help to understand this phenomenon if we draw a continuous line between extraordinary and everyday creativity. Gopi Krishna himself does not deny that *Kundalini* is at work in all men; but it is not streaming there, it is merely "dripping." Also, the physical sensations, which he himself has had, apparently do not normally occur in the creative process. Just as generally—except in a case like a headache—we do not think of the brain but of the thought, do not see the eye but what we have seen, so creativity as a rule is not aware of its organ. The unique aspect of Gopi Krishna's experience and of the whole school of Yoga to which his experience led him is the somatic awareness in oneself of a process of increasing consciousness. I am now returning to the justification for this somatic aspect, and I am raising the question of the phenomenological structure of creativity and also of its mental awareness by the self.

I would like to bracket this phenomenology between the poles of truth and process. On the one hand, each creative act confronts us with a truth; on the other hand, it occurs in some way in time.

The pole of truth corresponds to the teleological point of view that this and that understandable process *has* to occur when a truth is presented. Here we are again confronted with the polarity of the process of development, and we may thus include creativity under the concept of evolution to which we shall return in the next section.

In this sense each everyday learning experience is creative

33

for the respective individual, each production of a child's draw-
ing, a dress, a tool, each act of social encounter. Something irreversible occurs, a structure comes into being which now exists,
even if it is later destroyed. This structure has been meaningfully incorporated into a context of living and therein lies its
truth (truth is *adaequatio rei et intellectus* or the agreement
between actual fact and intelligible action). (Cf. my own book,
The Unity of Nature*, pp. 338-341.) We can understand its
process exactly insofar as we have previously had an understanding or are gaining an understanding through it of the
partial elements of environment and action which interact in it
(causality) and of the structural unity which arises in this in-
teraction (truth).

Let us speak specifically of rational understanding, particularly in the sciences. It is customary to present science as a
system of more or less logical inferences from either axioms
or experiences. That is the image of science as a fortress and
the way it is defended against criticism once it has been discovered. But it is not being discovered that way. It is a well-
known phenomenon in mathematics that one "sees" a theorem
prior to its proof, an intended structure prior to the formulated
sentence and seemingly incoherent segments of a proof prior
to the completed proof. In the empirical sciences Thomas Kuhn
(*The Structure of Scientific Revolutions***) has demonstrated the
leading role of paradigms which initially define what it is that
can be scientifically examined. An indivdual experience, then,
is nothing but a key on a keyboard we have built, which we
may press and whose selection we allow nature to make in the
process of questioning her. The archaeologist Ludwig Curtius's

---

*The Unity of Nature, by Carl Friedrich Freiherr von Weizsäcker; Carl Hanser
Verlag, Munich, 1971.
**The Structure of Scientific Revolutions, by Thomas Kuhn, the Chicago Uni-
versity Press, 1962.

last word was an admonition called out to a visitor in Rome who saw him in the day of his death: "And don't forget, one only sees what one knows." Science, according to Konrad Lorenz, is essentially the recognition of form, and this recognition of form is the nature of a creative act. We "make" the form by recognizing it; and we recognize it by making it.

From this point let us return to the level of "great" creativity. A great scientific discovery is the recognition of a particularly simple and fundamental form which heretofore had been hidden in a chaos of appearances and misunderstood theories. It is often described as an inspiration or a special gift of grace which comes to the researcher when and as it pleases, like an answer from "another authority" and then almost without effort on his part. It is never viewed as the inevitable result of his research effort. Here we find the often disturbing and happy experience: "It is not I; I have not done this." Still, in a certain way it is I—yet not the ego of will but of a more comprehensive self. Those who can sense this may find a like experience in ordinary thinking and acting: How little do we know of the conditions for the success of even the simplest thought, the simplest step or activity?

We can connect this experience of ego and self in two directions: We can follow Freud in his healing of neurosis or Gopi Krishna (and with him, for example, C. G. Jung) into mysticism. In the healing of neurosis I encounter something as nonego which I must acknowledge as ego in order to restore the unity of a torn consciousness. In scientific discovery I encounter something in my achievement which I must acknowledge as nonego and yet as myself. But the self is still hidden here from my consciousness and manifests itself only through the gift it has given me, through its achievement. In mysticism I must open myself to the self, I must overcome the ego, or what comes to the same thing, I must get to know my ego as a manifestation of the self. In the last analysis, I have to be the self which I have always been.

The negative also fits into this context. It manifests itself essentially as a victory of process over truth, as a "false truth" (*The Unity of Nature*, p. 339). This is already the case with the "healthy," but incomplete manifestations of the self, with "second best" achievements in the arts and sciences. The "idiocy of specialty" is the shadow of the sciences. Science knows each respective single part by achieving an objectivization, that is, a separation of a single part from the whole. With the concept of law it then restores the unity of the whole, but that restoration remains fragmentary. This opens up the possibility of a self-destruction of the scientific world. By analogy art also points towards life, but it cannot uphold life. The line, "the poet's eye, in a fine frenzy rolling" goes back to Plato's belief that the poets are given the power to utter truths under divine inspiration which they themselves as human beings do not understand. Even theories of art, which emphasize the craftsmanlike or conceptually objective in art, cannot deny—if they want to adhere to the truth—that art is an uncontrollable gift even in the hands of an old master who is certain of his craft. And those who know of the problems of an artist's life will probably not object to the thesis that an artist really cannot "live" in the proper sense of the term. He has been driven beyond the limits of normalcy by that which continuously happens in him without having found a firm place to stand in some other realm. An older friend, who first introduced me to the spiritual realm and who himself was an artist, once said, "Art is a substitute achievement. It is the action of a being who is not able to be." His opinion contradicts many current views and is eminently worthy of consideration!

The close relationship between genius and insanity is an old subject. We miss the significance of the connection, if in a "reductionist" fashion we assume that insanity, in one or more of its frequent forms, is considered as the primary phenomenon and if we then attempt to interpret personal genius in terms of its close relationship to insanity. In a sense, this repeats on a higher level an approach which Plato already attributed to Protagoras and which is represented today by Gehlen and others: namely, that man is an "imperfect being" in comparison with lower but more perfectly adapted animals. "The other way 'round the shoe is going to fit." Konrad Lorenz convincingly contends against the theory of an "imperfect being" that both physically and instinctively man is much better equipped than any other animal. Man's somatic and instinctive equipment is designed to serve an integrating intelligence. To express it in a stylized fashion: Man does not wear clothes because he has no hair, but he has no hair because he wears clothes. Hence, he is in bad shape if he should find himself without clothes. By way of analogy, Gopi Krishna points out the well-known fact that creative personalities—particularly in the religious area—generally possess greater gifts, such as intelligence, comprehension, and endurance, than the average person. But a partial failure of the integrating process leaves them, so to speak, without their proper clothing. Thus it may perhaps be possible to interpret psychotic processes in terms of those creative processes of which they are a distorted copy. At one time I was the addressee of the verbal torrent of a gifted young man who was probably in a schizophrenic state. I was able to "understand" every word. The complete material of genius was contained in these words, but was hopelessly deranged.

A similar judgment will have to be made about the relationship between drugs and mystical experiences. Drugs, then, would yield only a failing, unproductive fragment. I thought it particularly noteworthy how sharply Gopi Krishna, in his conversations, condemned any form of drug use, even as an "enticement" to meditation.

6. *What is Evolution?*

In the previous sections I have tried to present to the Western reader in as accessible a form as possible Gopi Krishna's thought and his conceptual and empirical material which, stemming from ancient India, often seems strange to us. A certain amount of "spoon-feeding" in the form of my own reflection on the material has been inevitable but this was included as a matter of service to the reader. This approach cannot go beyond an effort of submitting the author's theses for discussion and possible examination in accordance with his wishes. In the following I would at least like to indicate how I see these theses in relation to a philosophy of nature and history which I have been trying to develop from exclusively Western premises. Because of space limitations I have to express myself stenographically and, fully aware of the poor style this implies, refer the reader to my own publications.

The opposition of nature and history to designate the qualitative leap from the animal to man in my view constitutes a misleading conception. I prefer to speak of the "history of nature." In this I remain close to the concept of evolution for which, in the final analysis, Gopi Krishna as well as Aurobindo and Teilhard de Chardin are indebted to the evolutionism of the nineteenth century. The spiritualizing of this concept, which we find in all three of these thinkers, seems to me inescapable if man is included in evolution as the spiritual being he happens to be. At this point, however, there is the danger of a conceptual short circuit between vitality and spirit, which keeps many a critical mind from getting too close to this form of philosophy. Trusting in the Spirit which leads us into all truth, I therefore propose to proceed with extreme caution.

First, I do not share the hostility of all the spiritual evolutionists against Darwinism. It seems to me that we should not condemn the theory of selection but understand it.* According to that theory evolution, just like thermodynamic irreversibility, is based on the "historicity of time" which manifests itself among other things in the openness of the future and the accomplished fact of the past. The philosophical riddle is time; apart from it there is no need to introduce further riddles into an interpretation of evolution. Specifically, this means that the growth of the number and differentiation of forms does not only fail to contradict the second law of thermodynamics but that, under certain conditions which are fulfilled in the real world, the former may even be derived logically from the

*Cf. *The History of Nature,* lectures six to ten (Chicago, 1950); *The Relevance of Science,* Part I (London, 1964); *The Unity of Nature,* Part III (Munich, 1971).

latter.* We may say that the "energy" of evolution is nothing but the "flowing of time" itself viewed as the inescapability of the future. The "biologism" of the evolutionary thinkers then is nothing but the idea that the historicity of time manifests itself already in the organic sphere of life. Their "spiritualism" signifies, on the one hand, that even the spirit obeys the structure of time insofar as it appears in time. On the other hand, it implies the claim that time itself should be understood spiritually.

An approach in this direction is the attempt—which at first glance seems to lead in the opposite direction—of rendering visible the complete unity of nature by deriving biological concepts from physical concepts. The central concept in a logical analysis of this context is the concept of information. Virtual information is entropy. The growth of forms is a growth of virtual information, hence a growth of entropy. Molecular biology and cybernetics raise hopes for a reduction of biological to physical laws. But does not this elevate materialism to the throne?

The question is what we mean by "matter." For the physicist this can hardly be defined in terms other than "what satisfies the laws of physics." But what do the laws of physics tell us?

7. *Physics and Time*

Here I can only hint at an attempt to understand physics.** The reader, who considers this section a specialty, may pass it by.

* I hope to present an unpublished essay containing this sentence as part of a new book in the near future.
**Cf. *The Unity of Nature,* Parts II and III, 3; III, 5 (Munich, 1971) .

Physics as an empirical science historically develops into a unified theory. I think that we must find the reason why theory as such is possible in the unity of theory and that this unity, in turn, is based on conditions which make experience possible. Experience means learning from the past for the future. It is possible only in time. The structure of time is the basis of unity for physics. This structure must be conceptually analyzed by a logic of temporal propositions and a theory of probability as the form of an empirical prediction of the future. The use of the concept of probability in physics determines the structure of its two fundamental theories which are mutually related, quantum theory and thermodynamics. They are mutually related insofar as statistical thermodynamics presupposes an elementary theory and also because the concept of measurement in quantum theory cannot be explained apart from the thermodynamic concept of irreversibility. In a stage we have not yet reached these two theories therefore ought to merge into one. Finally, the flanking theories of the structure of space, of elementary particles, and of the universe ought to be derivable as the consequences of a semantically consistent interpretation of quantum theory. Here too, the basic approach is temporal, and I now call it temporal finiteness. Quantum theory is a theory of probabilistic prediction of decisions about contingent alternatives (measurements). Up to any given time only a finite number of alternatives are capable of being decided (the finite factualness of the past), but the number of future alternatives still to be decided is unlimited (openness of the future). This results at any given time in a finite-dimensional quantum theoretical phase space which may be represented by the smallest physical objects (elementary particles) in a compact, expanding regular space.

This hypothetical approach is philosophically significant because it accounts for all of physics as a theory of prognosticating the probability of alternatives which can be empirically decided. Even without any further hypothetical considerations it is clear that this falls within the scope of quantum theory. This is often considered a kind of observer-related subjectivism. On the other hand, this kind of physics is doubtlessly intersubjective: different observers can only have experiences which are mutually compatible, unless they are in error. We cannot think of a single observer for whom the future is factual. This "objective subjectivity" is denoted by the concept of information. Deriving the qualities of "matter" from a count of decidable alternatives may be expected to reduce the concepts of mass, energy, and information to a single unifying fundamental principle of moving form. In this view, the physical world would be—approximating Kant—that which can appear to a finite mind. Insofar as finite mind or consciousness is capable of appearing to itself empirically, it would itself constitute "matter." I have on occasion expressed this in a formula which follows Schelling: "Nature is spirit which does not have the appearance of spirit."

I do not ask the reader to accept these views. But the very fact that they are thinkable serves to demonstrate that the concept of *Prana* is not necessarily incompatible with our physics. *Prana* is spatially extended and vitalizing. Hence above all it is moving potency. The quantum theory designates something not entirely remote from this by the term "probability amplitude." The relationship may become clearer, when we consider probability as a strictly futuristic concept, that is, as the quantified expression of that towards which the "flow of time" is pressing to evolve. The view I have outlined eliminates the Cartesian split except where it presupposes separate subjects each with its own inherent objective consciousness. But when we hypothetically apply quantum theory to man, this exception will turn out to be less than absolute truth. Rather, it will prove to be a classical approximation without which the language of objectivization is impossible. That is to say, subject-object dualism prevails precisely in the approximation needed by subjects so that they can act and think in an objectivizing manner.

But can something, which is a prerequisite of objectivization, still be thought beyond objectivization? Can we think of a totality, which counts us among its parts, *as* a totality? We have reached the problem of the One.

8. *The One*

To make our approach let us first take a step backwards. Gopi Krishna claims that all reality is governed by one law and that this law is at the same time a biological and a spiritual law of evolution. We have expressed the view that the unity of physics as well as that of evolution may be deduced from the historicity of time and finally from a still unknown unity of time. What does unity really mean in this context?

Let us take a further step backwards. In quantum theory an object may be divided into constituent objects but it does not consist of them. This is demonstrated by the fact that an object permits different, conceptually incompatible divisions (expressed technically: different possible divisions of Hilbert space;

Einstein-Rosen-Podolsky-paradox). It is therefore a whole which does not consist of its parts, but rather loses its wholeness in the process of partition. Thus, the atom "is" not a system of nucleus and electrons; we only discover nucleus and electrons when we destroy the atom. Similarly, this table "is" not a structure composed of atoms. We only find atoms if we radically destroy the table. The area in which the concept of separate objects is valid is precisely the area of the classical approximation in which the "phase relationships" between objects ("their connections in the *Prana,*" if we may speak so recklessly) is considered negligible. If we now try to think of the whole world as a quantum theoretical object, then the world is not the multiplicity of objects it contains, but it divides into this multiplicity only for those who look at it with a multifariously objectivizing point of view.*

This is but one of the ways to approach the One; we might call it the physical-objective way. Plato, in the middle of the *Republic,* chooses a step-by-step progression from image to archetype. The Vedanta philosophy has thoroughly discussed the various possible approaches to the problem. If—in spite of the fact that I do not know Sanskrit—I may be permitted to give an opinion here, it would seem to me that Plato's mathematically trained mind reflects these problems even more precisely than does Indian thought. His *Parmenides* may be read like a preliminary sketch of all possible approaches to the problem and contains proof at the same time that none of them escapes contradiction. (It should be noted that the law of contradiction pre-

---

* Cf. the last essay in *The Unity of Nature,* Karl F. F. von Weizsäcker (Munich, 1971).

supposes a logic of at least two values and thus nonunity.) On the other hand, the Indian philosophy of the One can be understood only as a conceptual interpretation of the experience of meditation. Meditation leads to the experience of cosmic consciousness. I broke off at this point earlier, because we were no longer dealing with biography but with the subject matter itself; so the experience of stillness is the experience of self. It should be clear from all we have said that the way of meditation cannot be described theoretically.

9. *Christianity and History*

There are two questions I would still like to consider, if only in the brief form chosen here: The relationship of what we have said to Christianity and to our own future.

Gopi Krishna has the open attitude towards other religions characteristic of enlightened Hindus. Jesus Christ is for him one of the greatest, most compelling examples of religious genius. He uses the conversation of Jesus with Nicodemus as indicative of the meaning of the second birth, the birth from water and spirit. It is easy for modern intellectuals, who have no contact with the Church, to accept his openness, but this is much more difficult for the Christian theologian, and certainly not just on narrow confessional grounds. To be sure, it has been observed often enough that Christians get themselves into a kind of panic when they are asked to recognize the truth of other religions. Since intolerance, even purely intellectual intolerance against "unbelievers," is no longer persuasive these days, some Christians are still looking for the "ultimately decisive" difference between Christianity and the other religions.

I consider this anxious reaction (which in most instances is unaware of its anxiety) as unchristian and as a source of ever new and puzzling misconceptions about other religions and about one's own. It is an entirely different matter to make it clear that differentiations of the historical process cast the great religions and their founders into distinctly different roles and that this is the way it has to be. I caused surprise in Church circles when I said that belief in the Second Coming of Christ was part of Christianity.

At this point there are both a proper order of questioning and a proper division of duties for contemporary men, especially contemporary Christians. There are some convincing examples that an uprooted European or American may get firmer ground under his feet by becoming a Buddhist or a member of a Hindu community than by returning to the Christian Church or continuing his intellectual search. But these examples are in the minority. From a distance the exotic often appears more accessible, because we do not share the problems of its life. I would rather lead people back into the organized Church than out of it. But the idea that this can be justified on the grounds of an objective superiority of Christianity is self-delusion as long as we have not lived through what we have been discussing here. Moreover, that kind of justification is unnecessary.

There are, however, certain features of the Christian tradition we can already identify, which we have no reason to abandon. Foremost among them is the relationship of Christianity to temporal history. Indians, such as Gopi Krishna, have taken over part of secularized Christian thought in the form of the concept of evolution. Gopi Krishna is well aware of the fact that the worldliness of his concept of evolution places him in opposition to that aspect of the Hindu tradition which seeks only an ascent to and a permanent dwelling place in the One. The philosophy of open time is a Hebrew-Christian philosophy. To be sure, its relation to the One has remained completely unclear in the Christian theological-philosophical tradition. But when we equate that kind of time with the linear concept of time in chronological history and prognosis, then we have abandoned the level of asking necessary further questions. I do not have the solution to this problem but would like to see it kept before us in-the form of a question. The approach to an understanding of this question lies—as with all great theoretical questions—in the practical area. There is, of course, in Christianity also a proper place for contemplative minds. But only because they too, in their own way, share responsibility for the world and for each single living fellow man.

10. *The Future of Our World*

In the present volume Gopi Krishna merely hints at his expectations for the future. He expects that the present course of the world will lead to disaster, but that opening up a higher consciousness will result in better conditions for mankind and in real development. This pattern of expectation has often appeared during the course of history in a form suitable to the occasion, possibly because it has often been justified. I believe that it is certainly justified today. What counts is that we act in a world which justifies this kind of expectation. The question is how?

"If any man will do His will, he shall know of the doctrine . . . and ye shall know the truth, and the truth shall make you free."

St. John, Chaps. 7 and 8

PREFACE

ON THE BASIS OF MY OWN EXPERIENCE, extending to more than thirty years, I have come to the conclusion that mankind is slowly evolving towards a sublime state of consciousness of which fleeting glimpses have been afforded to us by all great seers and mystics of the past and present.

There is no doubt that some of the leading intellectuals of this era accept the existence of an evolutionary impulse in the race, but the ultimate goal and the modus operandi of the impulse—according to them—are still shrouded in mystery.

The purport of this work—which is only an introduction to the work that is to follow—is that there is a specific psychosomatic power center in man, and that it is by the action of this center that human evolution has proceeded so far. This Divine organ is naturally active in born sages, mystics, prophets, and all men of genius and can be roused to activity with appropriate methods in those already advanced on the ,path of evolution.

This power center, known in India by the name of Kundalini, has been used for the attainment of higher consciousness from times immemorial. In fact, there is every reason to believe that the extraordinary exuberance of religious genius in India in the Vedic Age—which was never surpassed in any subsequent epoch—was due to an intimate knowledge of this mighty mechanism, coupled with a social order more in harmony with evolutionary laws.

The existence of the power center and methods to rouse it were known in almost all ancient cultures of Asia, Europe, America, and even in Africa. I believe that a voluntary arousal of Kundalini, under satisfactory conditions and observed by competent investigators, can furnish *unquestionable proof* of the existence of this center in the body and its capacity to bestow psychic gifts, genius, and cosmic consciousness.

The experiments, when proved empirically, would effect a radical change in some current concepts about life and narrow the gulf existing between religion and science. It would also draw the attention of scholars towards the spiritual laws of evolution of which they have no knowledge at present.

In this brief summary the consequences of a collective breach of these laws are outlined. There is nothing haphazard and arbitrary in the universe, and there are as effective and as inviolable laws in the spiritual realm as there are in the physical world. The present explosive situation in the world is due to a serious violation of these laws.

At the present stage of evolution, the leading intellects of the earth—with proper efforts done in suitable environments—can in a fair percentage of cases succeed in arousing Kundalini and by this agency win access to a higher realm of consciousness. The supersensory plane of knowledge will be a necessary endowment of the luminaries who will guide the race in the foreseeable future.

It was the possession of this supersensory channel of cognition that gave to all great seers and prophets such deep knowledge of human nature and such farsightedness. The knowledge of the evolutionary laws and the goal of human progress bring to the forefront the need for mental hygiene as essential as the hygiene of the body. With the necessary precautions taken, it will be possible in the time to come, I believe, to control and eliminate war, just as mankind has already learned to control scourges such as cholera, plague, and smallpox.

Gopi Krishna
Srinagar, Kashmir—February, 1971

I.

THE SHORT FALL
OF RELIGION

THE PHENOMENON OF RELIGION IS A MYSTERY which so far has baffled all attempts toward a solution. There can be no denying the fact that from prehistoric times, as far back as modern investigators have been able to trace, man has always been in possession of a religion of some sort. Excavations of fossils of even the earlier Stone Age reveal ceremonial burials, thus furnishing evidence that, even in the primitive state of culture, belief in survival and the nature of the soul as an entity, separate and distinct from the body, was prevalent in various forms among the savage populations of the earth. From the study of primitive religions and cults, made by scholars, it is obvious beyond doubt that the savage faiths were more or less a bundle of superstition, myth, and ritual which not infrequently assumed horrible and fantastic form. Human sacrifice, sexual orgies, and dreadful forms of self-torture were not infrequently the common features of the methods of worship of these prehistoric creeds.

In less developed nations and even in some advanced societies we still come across surviving remnants of these hideous practices of the past. Until very recent times voluntary castration was prevalent among some categories of priests, and fearful instances of human sacrifice come every now and then to the notice of the shocked people of some countries. Among the isolated savage populations of Africa and Australia, the odious practices and rituals of primitive cults persist to this day. Not infrequently, revolting accounts of these quaint and repellent religious practices appear in well-known journals and newspapers of the world.

It is possible that the reader might be expecting something about the holy and the sublime, and my introduction of the subject by allusion to the hideous practices of the past might appear to some of them as ill-timed and irrelevant to the subject in hand. About this I wish to say that it is precisely because we have failed to study religion as a whole, from its earliest vestiges to the present lofty ideals of prophets and sages, not only in one but in all the religions of the earth taken as one composite whole, that we have so far not been able to discover the mighty law of nature underlying all the infinitely varied manifestations of religion and the religious impulse from prehistoric times to the present day. This law is as operative now, when the world is sharply divided between those who believe in the existence of God and those who do not, as it was when religion occupied a position of supremacy in many parts of the world, and even kings had to bow to the dictates of he Church.

I may be pardoned if I request the reader to put one simple question to himself: Why do we believe at all in the existence of an Omniscient and Omnipotent Divine Power that has brought this world and ourselves into existence, when we can find no evidence, perceptible to the senses, to prove conclusively that such a Power exists at all? And why do we strive for perfection and a better order of things when, from a study of the past and our own experience of the present, we are irresistibly drawn to the conclusion that from the earliest epochs not only the earth but even the seas have been a battleground for a ruthless struggle for existence in which neither God nor any supernatural agency ever intervened to grant victory or even protection to the believers against those who did not believe in God or a higher order of existence? The question I pose is as old as humanity itself, and to this day no satisfactorily convincing answer has been given by any authority on religion or by an illumined sage, ancient or modern. Had this question been effectively answered at any time in the long history of mankind, the division between believers and non-believers or between the devout and the skeptics would have ceased to exist; nor would religion have lost its ascendancy or suffered such reverses and upheavals as it has in this enlightened age.

It is now too late to ascribe all religious phenomena and the existence of the religious impulse in man to the Will of God as the preachers of religion often attempt to do. It is also too late to say that man is religious because God, who is pure spirit, is filled with desire that he should worship Him and seek Him

57

amid all the temptations of the flesh, in order to attain perennial peace and happiness in the Hereafter. The battle for salvation, which almost all religions of mankind impose on their followers, demands that the seeker must renounce the pleasures of earth to gain those of Heaven after death. But what the blessings of Heaven are and what exactly the state of man would be after his departure to the other world are enigmas that no one to this day has satisfactorily solved.

Even among orthodox believers of the various religions there is no concord as to what form the surviving soul would take after death to gain the promised reward for his heroic battle on earth against temptations to win access to God. Even the most eloquent writers on the subject are not agreed among themselves on this vital issue. Taking the Christian point of view, according to St. Paul, the soul wears a "celestial" or "spiritual" body in the other world as distinct from the "natural" and "terrestrial" body on the earth. "Flesh and blood cannot inherit the kingdom of God," he says. St. Augustine, however, declares that "in the resurrection the substance of our bodies, however disintegrated, shall be entirely reunited." He further clarifies this statement in these words: "Far be it from us to fear that the omnipotence of the Creator cannot, for the resuscitation and reanimation of our bodies, recall all the portions which have been consumed by beasts or fires, or have been dissolved into water, or have evaporated into the air."

Among modern writers also there is a grave divergence of opinion about this issue. "I believe in the resurrection of the flesh," says Bishop B. F. Westcott, "the flesh of which we speak as distinct to a resurrection is not that material substance which we can see and handle, measured by properties of sense." Dr. Fosdick affirms the persistence of the personality through death, but rejects the resurrection of the flesh, admitting, however, that he cannot easily imagine a completely disembodied existence. According to Dr. S. D. McConnel, the soul builds up, as it were, a brain within a brain, a body within a body, something like the "astral" body, which can persist after death. Bishop Manning is, however, more definite when he says, "When I enter there I shall be myself. This personality, these tempers and tastes, this character that I am forming here will be mine there. . . . I shall be seen as myself and shall be judged by what I am. I shall know my dear ones in the other life. I shall see and be seen. I shall speak and be spoken to." There are other views and opinions too. These citations have been reproduced as a sample to show that the state of man after death and the nature of the other world are still the objects of controversy and conflict of views even among the believers. *Where then lies the truth?*

The same divergence of opinion, in even a more prolific form, also exists among the Hindu authorities, both ancient and modern. According to Samkhya, there are innumerable souls which on embodiment are ruled by Karma from birth to birth. According to Shankara, every human soul is Brahman itself, indivisible and entire, oblivious in embodied life to His sovereign nature under the influence of Maya, an unexplainable conditioning factor which brings the whole creation into existence not as a cosmic reality but as an illusory appearance. Ramanuja, another famous philosopher, opposes this view and holds that the soul, or Jiva, is not identical with Brahman but subordinate to it. Swami Dayananda, a modern sage, believes, on the strength of Vedas, in the existence of innumerable spirits or souls who bear the fruit of Karma from birth to birth, until they attain liberation by righteous actions and worship of God.

The views expressed about the Hereafter and the nature of the Soul are almost as varied as there are sects or creeds in India. There are many who after the death of a person prescribe monthly or yearly ceremonies, known as Sraadha, in which offerings of food, drink, and apparel are made to the priest, who performs the ceremonies, in the belief that they reach the departed souls in the other world. There are other authorities for whom such ceremonies are not only useless but even constitute a flagrant violation of common sense.

In Islam too there is great diversity of views about the conception of the Hereafter. According to some authorities, the righteous soul after death comes to God and lives in blissful proximity to Him, while according to others he first enjoys the reward of his meritorious deeds in a delightful paradise. According to one school of Buddhism, there is no immortal soul, persisting unaltered through the endless circle of births and deaths, but rather the human personality is the result of an aggregation of material elements, known as skandhas, which persist as an integrated unit of life by the force of Karma, disintegrating again at the time of final dissolution, or Nirvana, on the expiry of past Karma brought about by a righteous way of life.

Others believe in an individual soul and its persistence through the dreary circle of births and deaths. Taoists have other views, and Zoroastrians still other. It is needless for our purpose to recapitulate all of them. Suffice it to say that there are almost as many views about God, Soul, and the Beyond as there are faiths and creeds in the world. This at the present state of man's knowledge and achievements is a very unsatisfactory state of affairs; as incommensurate with his mental stature as the stories of fairies and gnomes, appearing real to children, are for adult minds.

I should like it to be borne in mind that I am not pointing out these discrepancies in the religious beliefs of various faiths of mankind with any intent of criticism, as I hold religion and, in general, every healthy faith in such esteem and reverence that even the thought of destructive criticism would not enter my mind, but it is absolutely necessary to point out this variation to bring into prominence the errors that have been made in dealing with what is perhaps the most powerful incentive to noble effort in the heart of man. There are variations not only in the conceptions of the Soul and the Beyond, but also in the gospels of various faiths. Not infrequently the revealed teachings and commandments of one creed flatly contradict those of another, although both claim their origin from the same Divine Source. Is it possible that the Author of this vast Creation can be so variable and fanciful that He would say one thing to one, another to a second and yet another to a third and so on, thereby inciting one to fight the other on the basic issues of life and death?

There are many exponents of faith who gloss over these glaring discrepancies, arguing that every teaching is meant for a particular place, time, and people, the incongruities between them being inevitable. In their zeal to justify the stand that all these Revelations have emanated from God, they forget the obvious truth that there are divergences even in respect of basic issues, as for instance the nature of Soul, the concept of the

Ultimate, the ideas about the Afterlife, and so on, which, being eternal Truths, could not have one form for a Hindu, another for a Christian, another for a Zionist, another for a Muslim, and an altogether different form for a Buddhist.

When in the case of physical knowledge, gathered by the puny, fallible intelligence of man, there is uniformity in our ideas about the shape of the earth, the phases of the moon, movements of the heavenly bodies, the nature of tides, the distance of the sun and moon, the flow of blood or the like—in which the variations, if any, are extremely slight—is it not inconceivable that the Revelations made directly by the Infallible Source of all Knowledge and Wisdom, the Lord God Himself, should be so conflicting and self-contradictory about the fundamental concepts of faith, which are not possible of verification by our senses and the mind? Not only this but some of the Revelations, as for instance those dealing with cosmogonic issues and the Origin of Man, are found to be mythical and erroneous when studied in the light of the discoveries made by science.

We cannot also ignore the fact that every major faith is split up into numerous sects and creeds; and each of these divisions has its own ideas and concepts, differing from each other, but all founded on the authority of the Revealed scriptures, interpreted diversely to support the views expressed by the Founder of each sect. "Diverse are the Vedas [revealed scriptures] and diverse the Smritis [manuals of law]," says Mahabharata. "No sage was ever born who did not found a new creed. The essence of Dharma is shrouded in mystery. That by which great men travel becomes the Path." This ancient observation is applicable to any religion and faith and to any epoch of time. There has been, perhaps, no period in the history of mankind when there were so many cults and creeds and such a diversity of views about the Soul and God as exists in this enlightened age.

The main reason for this schismatic tendency in the domain of faith is that there is no unanimity of thought among the adherents of various faiths as well as among the adherents of each major faith. This diversity of views, in turn, springs from the blatantly obvious fact that the law underlying spiritual phenomena and the religious impulse in man has so far baffled all efforts to understand it. It is easy to infer, when viewed in the light of the fact that the physical universe is rigidly bound by laws from the movements of atoms to those of colossal suns and nebular systems, that there must also be a similar coherence and consistency in the spiritual realm.

It is also obvious that the human intellect, which discerns order in the cosmos, both in its tiniest fragments and the whole, cannot itself be devoid of system and law. It is deplorable that our present concepts about religion and its Founders savor of irrationality for the simple reason that when we hold that God himself revealed a certain gospel to a particular individual, in exclusion of the rest, we at once attribute nepotism and partiality to a system of existence ruled by inviolable laws from one end to the other.

There was a time when no thinker, however great, had the temerity to question the accounts of creation and cosmogony contained in the scriptures. This was not restricted to one faith but applied to all the religions of mankind. We are all aware of the historical instance when Galileo, white-haired and bent with age, was made to recant his monumental discoveries in the realm

of astronomy by the dignitaries of the Church. Stringent pun-
ishments and the severest public opprobrium awaited those in
India who dared to infringe upon the caste restrictions. Al-Hallaj
suffered martyrdom for giving honest expression to his own remarkable spiritual experience, similar to that of many Yoga
saints, because it was not in conformity to the orthodox faith.
There can be no greater disservice to mankind at this crucial
state than to belittle the decisive role played by religion in keeping man on the path of virtue and in diverting his thought to
noble and sublime ideals of existence; but at the same time there
can be no greater betrayal of the trust reposed by the masses in
those who profess knowledge of the Occult and the Divine than
to ignore the need of the time, demanding investigation of the
laws underlying religious experience and phenomena, as has
been done with signal success in respect to the phenomena of
the physical world.

We are face to face with a colossal problem when we try to
knit together the infinitely scattered threads of religion, say from
the time of Moses to the present day. There is such a huge mass
of literature, said to have emanated in part from God, and there
are so many varied points of view that it appears impossible to
untie the tangled skein and to locate the thread which now by
winding and twisting reflects the appearance of an inextricably
confused mass. It is needless for me to say that the difficulties I
have pointed out in understanding the mysteries of religion and
in lending belief to the various dogmas and beliefs have been
felt by the majority of intelligent people at one time or another,
though they often refrain from giving expression to their feelings
for various reasons. A large part of them stifle their doubts and

misgivings to avoid the adverse opinion of those who believe implicitly in faith, while others, swayed by sentiment, feel reluctant to cast doubts on the ideas and beliefs held by their parents and forebears for centuries, and yet others continue to attend the Church and temple more to observe a formality than to satisfy a deep yearning of the heart that comes from a firm conviction in the tenets of a faith.

Frankly speaking, the intellectual stature of the average man has grown so high, as compared to his prototype of a few centuries ago, that the beliefs and dogmas of faith which instantly appealed to the latter now fall flat on the ears of the former. While there can be no gainsaying the fact that various religions of mankind, even in their present form, have a strong appeal for millions upon millions of their followers and keep alight the flame of spiritual knowledge even at this time, we cannot ignore the equally, if not more, important aspect of the matter that every fresh addition to the knowledge of mankind in the realms of biology, cosmogony, or psychology steadily adds to the ranks of the skeptics year after year until a time is reached when the present-day organized religions are reduced to mere skeletons, incapable of making any impact on the multitudes.

I am sure that the leaders of religious thoughts of all denominations visualize this catastrophe but feel themselves helpless to prevent it. We have already seen with pain how but one stroke of revolution swept away nearly every trace of organized religion from the countries which came under its effect, with the result that, in the short span of half a century, the intelligentsia of these lands are now as antagonistic to the idea of God and the basic tenets of religion as they were in favor of them before.

II.

THE ERROR OF SCIENCE

ADDRESSING MYSELF NOW MORE PARTICULARLY TO THE SCIENTISTS
and scholars, I may be permitted to say that there is absolutely no
reason for self-complacency, much less for pride, in the thought
that the intellectual efforts of the past two or three centuries
have culminated in a vast increase in human knowledge, in a
remarkable leap forward in technology, in political freedom, in
the conquest of disease, victory over famines and progress in
other directions conducive to the peace and happiness of mankind. I have purposely employed a note of caution for the reason
that there are still large gaps in our knowledge, especially in the
knowledge of human mind, which if not filled up, at least to the

extent possible now, might result in undoing in a day all that has been achieved with the sweating labor of hundreds of years.

Leaving apart the lacunae in our knowledge of the physical universe—the increasing problems posed by astronomy, the real nature of time and space, the basic substance of the nebulae or the ultimate form of matter—it is no exaggeration to say that our present knowledge of the mind and its instruments, the brain and the nervous system, is still in its infancy, utterly insufficient as compared to the information we have gathered about the physical world. This disproportion in the knowledge of the two worlds in which we live, the outer and the inner, makes us a giant in one direction and a dwarf in the other, a clear sign of abnormality that can only have serious repercussions on our thoughts and actions, and thereby on our whole life and the environment that we create for ourselves.

If we have not so far realized the obvious truth that the zest for life and the happiness of mind flow from the inner fountain of our being and not from our material possessions, then we are still lacking in the proper understanding of our own nature. The birds in the air and the beasts in the forests live joyously and contentedly in the environment provided by nature. Because of his more developed nervous system and brain, and a more sensitive, unprotected flesh, man needs some amenities, it is true—wholesome food, shelter, and dress—but beyond these basic needs he does not depend much on his outer belongings for the possession of a joyous inner world.

Let us examine this issue a little more in detail. Can there be any denial of the historic fact that for the past thousands of years a vast majority of the race has drawn consolation and solace at times of acute mental distress and despair, found inspiration and guidance at times of darkness and doubt, gained relief from pain and suffering, obtained peace in sorrow and grief, contentment in penury and want from the recorded or orally transmitted utterances of some famous men and women, whose needs were few and earthly possessions meagre but whose inner fount was so full of the greatest treasures and the noblest attributes of life that to this day they prove an inexhaustible source of strength and happiness for millions upon millions of human beings? When we look at the simple lives of the Founders of all major faiths, the Biblical prophets, the seers of the Upanishads, Socrates and Confucius or others, and the environments that surrounded them, we cannot resist the conclusion that luxury and overabundance are not at all necessary for the bloom of the inner man. From the experience of the past we can even say that their absence is more in harmony with the still unknown laws that govern the moral and spiritual development of man.

Can we deny that even the highest intellects of this age, men and women whose names are household words, at times of mental conflict much more prevalent now than it was ever before, continue to draw inspiration and strength from the lives and utterances of these simple, unassuming thinkers of the past? If not, is it not a matter for serious thought, much more serious than has ever been devoted to it? If with all our marvellous achievements in technology, tremendous advances in the arts and sciences, and the provision of undreamed of luxuries and amenities we have failed in this glamorous age to produce even a few men and women, commanding the same stature, intellectual, moral, and spiritual, as was attained by most of these historical figures of the dim past in environments of ignorance, hardship, and want, there must be something wrong with our own notions about human life and our own ideas about the measures needed and the environments necessary for the proper and harmonious development of man. How can any planning done in the present or the future prove fructuous unless we draw a lesson from this experience of the past and try to locate the serious gap in our knowledge that is making us progressively richer outside without adding a tithe to our treasure within? On the other hand, if we take stock of the world round us, we cannot fail to notice glaring signs and symptoms of inner poverty that is rapidly transforming mankind into a live volcano which with the least accident or indiscretion can burst to spread complete devastation not only on itself but on every form of life inhabiting the earth.

Toward the end of the nineteenth century, Professor Tyndall made what he thought was a remarkable statement when he said that he could see the possibilities of life in matter. Before him stalwarts like Cabanis, Buchner, Hobbes, Priestley, Comte, Mill, Herbert Spencer, Heckel, Karl Marx, and after them Freud, Santayana, John Dewey, Bertrand Russell, and others with all the power of their genius in their own particular spheres of thought directly or indirectly denied independent existence to life and consciousness. The influence of their thought persists to this day on the thinking of the scholars of our time, with the result that but few scientists of repute have the inclination to associate themselves openly with societies or groups interested in the occult and the supernatural. The irony is that all these mighty edifices of materialistic or agnostic thought have been built up when matter itself is still a riddle and when nothing positive is known about the nerve impulses, about psychic energy, and about the bewildering activity of the nervous system and the brain. In the ancient civilizations of Greece and India atheists and agnostics flourished side by side with sages and visionaries, as incisive in their analysis and as logical in their arguments as are their counterparts today, but they never were able to stifle the deep-seated urge in the human heart that finds expression in religious ideas and acts.

No one can deny the greatness of these brilliant luminaries of the past, but at the same time no one can deny that some of the basic concepts about mind and matter on which they built their towering structures are now decade after decade eroded by fresh waves of thought, and the day is not distant when with complete erosion they will crumble down, surviving only as curious relics of a less informed past.

What are the fruits of this overemphasis on the soma, on unrestricted material amenities, on luxurious living, on the race for possession and power, and on the denial of the spiritual nature of man, or the independent existence of consciousness or an Almighty, Intelligent Cause of the universe we see around us? Has the human race become more noble, more happy, and more peaceful than it ever was in the past or do we notice ominous fissures and cracks in the huge mass that threaten an immediate collapse, and are not these ominous signs also in evidence in the wealthy, advanced nations at the zenith of material prosperity, surrounded by a plethora of all the lavish blessings provided by science? What inner torment drives millions upon millions of young men and women to seek solace in hallucinatory drugs, in ceaseless smoking, in alcohol, while millions more, tired of ordered life, roam from place to place as hippies and tramps, as rebels to society, often in a state of total abandonment, utterly indifferent to the rules of conduct and modes of behavior that are sacrosanct for the elder generations? Why do millions more in all walks of life take to occult practices, to spiritualism, to astrology, asceticism, to Yoga and the like, in unprecedented numbers in an effort at self-transcendence to find answers to questions that no amount of temporal knowledge can answer or to assuage a hunger that no hoard of material wealth could ever satisfy in the past? Can we shut our eyes to the glaring fact that in no period of history, even during the darkest age, were there such atrocities, such wholesale massacres, such hideous wars, and such bloody revolutions as this century has witnessed? And after witnessing all this horror, is there a single country or a single nation on earth that does not prepare for war? Or is there any that is not every now and then torn by internal dissension or shaken by revolts, upheavals, and bloodshed that make a stable environment or a regular life well nigh impossible?

I am not in any way attempting to paint a gloomy picture of the over-all condition of the modern world. Flagrant disregard of moral values, indecency, indiscipline, violence, sexual delinquency, and the like have assumed a position of ascendancy that is grossly reflected in most of the newspapers and periodicals of the day. Before the very eyes of many of those whose writings or discourses dismantled the walls that were erected by faith to keep man from yielding completely to the animal in him—time-honored conventions, higher rules of conduct, chivalrous ideas, the ideals of family life, affection and love, chastity and rectitude, altruistic and philanthropic zeal, lofty codes of honor—all those sublime attributes of character that distinguish man from the beast—are crumbling to dust amid the laughter and derision of the nihilists and the Antichrist. The last days of the Romans, the most luxurious nation the world ever saw, were marked by certain characteristics, mentioned by historians, which can serve as a warning about the fate in store for the glamorous civilization of our time. They were: (1) The breakdown of the family, (2) The mounting craze for pleasure, (3) Extravagant spending, (4) Expanding armies and constant threat of attacks, (5) Depreciation of moral values, (6) Decay in religion, (7) Political instability and (8) Immoderate sex.

Considered in the light of this fact, who can doubt that modern society is rapidly heading toward the same ignominious end, and the ominous signs and symptoms that cause some degree of alarm in the sober and the sage are but the forerunners of serious calamities to come? It is a historical fact that no once victorious nation and no once powerful dynasty of kings in the past ever came to a realization of the fact, when degeneration set in, that they were decaying and rapidly rolling down the slope, until one day they landed in the mire at the base. On the other hand, they ascribed their growing problems and troubles to their enemies, oblivious to the fact that the real enemies were their own fast deteriorating minds. The writers, thinkers, rulers, spiritual heads, and scholars of today, irrespective of the country or the nation to which they belong, seldom realize that by conforming to the taste and choice of the masses they cannot arrest the process of decay, for the reason that degenerative tendencies in art, literature, philosophy, social customs, national character, moral values, and even in religion remain unnoticed by those who fall victims to senescence.

While the leaders of religious thought continue to dwell on the blessings of faith, both from the pulpit and in the press, in masterly works and discourses, the ranks of unbelievers continue to swell or new creeds and cults continue to spread, leading to chaos and confusion which become more confounded every day. In the same way, the politicians haranguing on peace see violence growing apace, and the moralists, lauding the path of virtue, watch in despair the advancing tide of immorality, powerless to stop it.

What has suddenly gone wrong with the world? Why do the erudite find themselves powerless to cope with the growing spate of violence, discontentment, and disaffection spreading on all sides? The Communist countries are as much flooded by it as the rest of the world. Even an optimist like Julian Huxley has had to admit that there is a bright future for humanity provided it does not destroy itself in a nuclear war. This is the frame of mind of most other thinkers and scientists as well. But why this pessimism? Why are the promises held by science and technology proving to be a source of worry and fear rather than that of elation and joy? And this is just the beginning. What will be the aftermath of the third World War, if it is fought? Do not all signs and portents point to the conclusion that sooner or later a global conflagration is inevitable? What will be the condition of humanity when, devastated by nuclear blasts, a battered and broken remnant survives, amid the ruins of modern civilization, to carry on the task of history? Can anyone provide answers to these questions, and can anyone visualize to what harvest the present waves of unrest, revolt, violence, bloodshed, depravity, and disorder would lead? If not, does it not mean that the fate of mankind hangs by a thread, and all the resources and ingenuity of the race are now powerless against the threatening monster that has been raised, and that for this we can only blame the faulty thinking and planning of the architects of the modern world?

It is not correct to say that this discordance is due to the transition from an agrarian to an industrial state of society or from a rural to a predominantly urban life, surrounded by conveniences provided by advanced technology, and that a certain duration of time would be needed for mankind to adjust to it. It is equally wrong to say that all these unhealthy reactions —violence, war, revolt, delinquency, drugs, and the like—are the outcome of lack of adjustment on the part of individuals to their unconscious urges and impulses that are normally suppressed. Equally incorrect is the argument of the men of faith that all these evils are the inevitable fruit of heretical tendencies and the revolt of reason against God. The stand that vice and wickedness were always present in human nature and they appear more widespread now, as they are coming out more in the open, owing to the present greater freedom of thought and act, is equally fallacious. Experience of the past does not support any of these arguments. Barring the one single factor of the influence of modern technology, which alone cannot be so pernicious, all the other factors (urbanization, suppression of unconscious urges, heresy, and unfettered freedom of thought and action) also operated in the past without causing such explosive situations—social, moral, and political—as we are witnessing now. Social, moral, and political evils assumed overwhelming proportions only when a nation or people, through a wrong mode of life and thought, fell victims to decay, a grim process of inner deterioration leading finally to senescence and death—the award of Heaven on a collective breach of evolutionary Laws. *This is the verdict of history.*

The greatest tragedy of our time has been that, carried away by the overwhelming impact of important discoveries made in the domain of science, the thinkers of this age, believing that they had found solutions to most of the riddles that confronted them, gave expression to views about the various facets of human life, about the hopes and aspirations of man, about his mind and spirit, about the aim of his existence, about this world and the Hereafter, which in many important respects are as incorrect as were the concepts of the ancients about the physical world. The gravest error in this assessment has been the summary dismissal of religion and the supernatural as a phenomenon not verifiable through the methods adopted by science and, therefore, not worthy of inclusion in the province of scientific research. One of the main reasons responsible for this uncompromising attitude of science toward religion rests partly on the dogmatic attitude of the custodians of faith themselves, insisting on blind acceptance of the teachings contained in the gospels of a creed, and partly on the exaggerated stress on divine intervention and theophany that characterizes more or less all the religions of mankind.

A more considerate assessment, however, would not have omitted to take cognizance of the fact that there is no other single factor, including politics, that had such an influence on the life of man from the remotest antiquity to the present day as religion has wielded, and no other factor that has contributed so richly to the growth of civilization and culture as it has done. An institution or a bent of mind that has persisted for thousands of years in all the vicissitudes through which mankind passed could not rest on mere fancy or delusion or fraud or a bubble created by the priests, but on something more solid existing in the mental fabric of man. It certainly could not be a pathological or hysterical affection for the reason, firstly, that in such a case it could not have persisted through all the stages of human growth from the most primitive to the present civilized state and, secondly, if such were the case, then it means that the loftiest men ever born had this mental kink in a more acute form than is the case with men in general. Such a premise, in turn, would lead to the preposterous conclusion that the highest achievements of thought with respect to the nobler aims of life are only possible in a disordered condition of the human brain.

That prejudice has been the main cause responsible for this failure to investigate one of the most prevalent and most constant phenomena of the human mind is obvious. Even a casual study of the major faiths of mankind could not fail to bring home to any unbiased scholar that, according to all schools of religious thought, a certain prescribed way of life and conduct and certain prescribed mental and physical disciplines can act as a ladder to lead earnest seekers to God or to states of consciousness in which communion with Divinity becomes possible. This systematization of religious effort to gain sublime objectives is at least as old as history, and no doubt was practiced in almost all countries under the sun. The religious lore of India is especially rich in this respect, and it is not at all difficult, even for a casual observer, to see that from time immemorial hundreds upon hundreds of highly venerated sages and seers bore irrefutable testimony to the efficacy of the various methods and disciplines prescribed for the purpose of granting the spiritual insights and the supernormal gifts associated with religion in any form. Later, these methods and disciplines came to be known under the generic name of Yoga, and under this appellation continue to this day. During recent years, Shri Ramakrishna, Maharishi Ramana, and Sri Aurobindo, three outstanding products of this ancient culture, also bore unreserved testimony to the efficacy of these systems and the extraordinary experiencs that flow from them.

The most rational way to attest to the truth of religion, and to accept or reject its claims, was to test these practices and disciplines after making a comparative study of all the systems in existence in different parts of the earth, and then to pronounce a verdict on the basis of the results achieved. But to this day it was never done by any group of scientists, dedicating their life to this research alone, in the same way that innumerable groups and societies are doing in respect to the still unexplained riddles of the physical world. The decision to ignore the claims of faith and to refuse its admission into the province of science was thus taken without trial, a most unscientific way of dealing with an obstinate phenomenon of this type. The Society for Psychical Research came into existence to investigate another category of phenomena, relating to paranormal manifestations in certain specially gifted individuals, which are not explainable in terms of the known laws of science. Even this research, undertaken in a skeptical environment, yielded valuable information and proved decisive in establishing the validity of telepathy or, in other words, the possibility of communication between two minds directly without any known interconnecting medium to make the communication possible. Premonition, prophesy, and clairvoyance, though not conclusively proved, showed a high degree of probability, and the weight of evidence in respect to physical phenomena — telekinesis, levitation, materialization, etc. — was such that the possibility could not be ruled out altogether.

But there was no investigation of the possibilities offered by religion itself. The utterances of the spiritual luminaries of the past, treated with great reverence for thousands of years, were rejected outright without trial. It became the fashion to explain the phenomena of mind in terms of atoms and molecules composing the matter of the brain. The more sanguine are looking forward to the day when they can manipulate the genes to produce human embryos at will. Others visualize the production of test-tube babies at not too distant a date. Every word that a scientist writes is to be accepted as gospel truth. But every word in a scripture is to be viewed with doubt and distrust. The wheel of fortune that once gave such ascendancy to faith that it became the sole arbitrator of what a man should believe or not believe, irrespective of the evidence of his senses and the judgment of intellect, now turning round has reversed the position and made reason the arbitrator, alas, to be guilty of the same abuse. The summary condemnation of religion as unworthy of attention of men of science, as time will show, has been one of the most colossal blunders ever made by man, because under the loose and sometimes fantastic dress, worn by faith, lies concealed the greatest secret of existence, which rules the fate of mankind in the same way that the gravitational pull of the sun governs the rotation of the earth.

The ancient scriptures of India, studied with attention, will be found to be full of references to this still unknown Spiritual Law. The entire religious literature of the world will be found to be an expression of this mighty Law, intuitively grasped by the prophets and sages of the past. Not only in the Shruti (that is, the revealed scriptures, for example, the Vedas) but also in the Smritis (the manuals of Law) and in the Puranas (that is, mythology) the nature of this Law and its implications and possibilities are discussed again and again, embellished with supernatural accounts and episodes which prevent the uninitiated from reaching the solid core. There is undeniable evidence to show that this secret was initially discovered in some remote civilization prior to the entry of Aryans into India, for there are unmistakable signs to show that it was known to the denizens of the Indus Valley civilization three thousand years before the birth of Christ. To avoid ambiguity, I should like to say at once that it is a biological Law, as possible of demonstration in a laboratory as the flow of blood. The tragedy is that the specialists and the scholars of today treat the human brain like a sealed compartment, as circumscribed in its performance as the brain of an animal. Although there is undeniable evidence to show that in certain specially constituted individuals, as for instance in the case of mediums and sensitives, mystics and seers, child prodigies and even men of genius, the normal human limit is exceeded to an amazing extent, in a manner for which there is no satisfactory explanation from the side of science, the scholars, moving in the same old rut, continue to harp on the bewildering complexity of the brain and the enormous number of brain cells as a sufficient cause to account for any paranormal phenomena exhibited by man. This means, in other words, that scientists of this category are adopting the same dogmatic attitude towards the still inexplicable phenomena of mind as ecclesiastical pundits adopted towards the unintelligible physical phenomena a few centuries ago.

III.

EVOLUTION IS
THE ANSWER

THE OBVIOUS EXPLANATION THAT THE HUMAN BRAIN is still in a state of evolution and that these extraordinary phenomena, witnessed in these uncommon men and women, are but the erratic manifestations of a higher state of consciousness that will be the natural possession of the man of the future may still not find favor with the biologist, but this explanation provides complete corroboration for and squarely fits in with his own theories about the origin of man. The phenomena are erratic and often beyond the control of the individuals themselves, for the simple reason that there is still a wide gap between the present condition of the human brain and the ultimate state of perfection it has to reach when only these, what we call supernatural or paranormal, gifts can become the normal possession of at least the fully evolved members of the human race. Until that time, in the great majority of those who are born with these talents as a natural heritage, we can reasonably expect only imperfect, erratic, or abortive exhibitions, as we see in mediums, psychics, and even in some categories of mystics on account of the fact that the combination of circumstances and the eugenic factors involved cannot but continue to remain faulty in the present state of society, now in utter ignorance of this mighty Law. There is, however, no doubt that by an incredible combination of factors finished specimens of the perfect man of the future were born at rare intervals, as in the case of Buddha, Christ, Vyasa, and others, who, endowed with a superior type of consciousness and in possession of paranormal gifts, amazed their contemporaries with their extraordinary psychical and intellectual talents which the latter, ignorant of the Law, ascribed to special prerogatives from God.

The same phenomenon must have been repeated during the period of transition of the anthropoid into man, and abortive, unfinished specimens of the intelligent man of the future must have begun to appear now and then. They exceeded the highest limit of the general mental level of the sub-man, until finally the transition was complete, having been assisted from time to time by the superior contributions of the latter for more healthful ways of life and better organization of society. From the dawn of history, the illuminati effected a better organization of human life and society in much the same way by their example and precept to facilitate the process of evolution until the summit is reached. The explanation for the amazing tenacity with which mankind has held fast to the teaching of prophets and sages, even at the cost of widespread bloodshed and suffering—a mysterious phenomenon that has defied all attempts to find a rational solution so far—lies in this, that the teaching in one form or another, to a greater or lesser extent, contains precious hints about the mode of life and the organization of society necessary to meet the demands of the evolutionary impulse still active in the race. This teaching, emanating from exalted states of consciousness, the natural endowment of the man of the future, seeing further ahead than the intellect, was accepted as Revealed, since it is not the product of a normal mind, but of a consciousness still far beyond the capacity of the normal human brain.

In dealing with religion and every supernormal manifestation of the human mind we are, therefore, dealing with the phenomenon of evolution, in extremely rare cases resulting in the appearance of men and women who exhibit in a miniature or imperfect form one or more of the extraordinary talents that would be the normal adornment of the future man. In all probability, in the prehistoric days in India or even in some earlier culture, the symptoms attending the abnormal conditions of mystics and mediums were carefully studied by their contemporaries to understand the reasons for the extraordinary states. The usual explanations that the manifestations were the result of the possession of the individuals by a spirit or demon or a divine being, even when readily accepted, still left the primitive inquirers wondering how such possession could occur; and naturally the physical symptoms which attended the manifestations must have been observed with equal care to find the secret of the strange exhibitions, showing possession of powers and gifts entirely beyond the capacity of the average man. The most common feature of this mystical phenomena, entrancement, is often exhibited in varying degrees by mediums also. According to the observation of Meyers, "during the trance, breathing and circulation are depressed. The body is more or less cold or rigid, remaining in the same position which it occupied at the oncoming of the ecstasy, however difficult and unnatural this pose may be. . . . A swoon-like condition is also present among certain types of hysteria as also among mediums and sensitives during seances." It is easy to imagine that time and again the more enterprising among the primitive observers of these strange exhibitions must have tried to induce the same psycho-physiological conditions in themselves—insensibility, diminished breathing, and a cataleptic condition of the body—with the aid of different methods in which restraint of breathing (in imitation of the born cases), now known as Pranayama, must have played a prominent part. During the course of these amateurish trials, a most remarkable coincidence must have occurred somewhere with the appearance of the strange phenomena in one already mature to some extent for the experience, resulting in the discovery of one of the greatest secrets of nature hidden in the body of man. That secret is Kundalini.

Space does not permit me to dwell on this discovery in detail. For a further exposition of all the available material several volumes would be needed, which will appear from time to time. Suffice it to say here that this fabulous Power Reservoir, referred to in the Vedas, the oldest recorded religious scriptures in the world, as Gayatri, the cornerstone of every spiritual and occult practice and the one, single source of all mystical experience and paranormal phenomena, has been the most sought after object of quest in India for the past thousands of years. Adept after adept in unambiguous terms has testified in recorded confessions to the existence and efficacy of this marvellous psychosomatic Power-Mechanism with awe and adoration, and has treated it as an All-Intelligent and Omnipotent Divine Energy, the architect of every form of life in the universe. What is of particular interest, with special relevance to the problems of this age, is the fact that in hundreds of these writings the biological reactions, caused in the body on the arousal of the Power Center, have been described in unmistakable terms, the best that general level of knowledge of those days allowed the authors to do. They provide important clues for the modern investigator who has even a passing knowledge of physiology. These accounts are so numerous, so consistent, so unmistakably pointing to the same experience, despite variations in time and place, and often so sincere in their expression it is a wonder that the momentous nature of the discovery has escaped the keen eyes of the modern scholars, both of the East and the West, who studied and translated some of these works.

Although a good deal of the intricate mechanism of the human body has become known through the laudable efforts of modern savants, it is still an unfathomed mystery, even to the most erudite scholars of our age. The province of thought especially is still the most inscrutable realm of all. So deep is the mystery and so unprepared for the disclosure are the learned that hardly anyone would be ready to believe the amazing truth, that as a measure of evolution a subtle process is at work in the average human body, resulting in the formation of a biochemical essence

85

of a volatile nature that can be readily transformed into a psychic radiation of high potency. From a rational point of view no un-biased man of science should feel incredulous of such a possi-bility, for the simple reason that in every form of life the produc-tion of nerve and psychic energy is constantly going on to feed the brain and the nervous system, although the manner in which this is effected, the nature of the energies and the method of their formation from the gross ingredients of the organism are yet not known to science. What I affirm is that the process of evolution leads to the production of a more potent form of those biochemi-cal substances that act as fuel for psychic energy in its various forms. It would be ridiculous to contend that the most elaborate chemical laboratory on earth, that is, the human body, cannot readily manufacture a substance of this nature, under the influ-ence of evolutionary impulses active in it. In an infinitesimal dose of a three hundred thousandth part of a gram, equal to a speck of dust, lysergic acid, diethylamide, popularly known as L.S.D., creates a revolution in human consciousness, and may even lead in rare cases to insanity, suicide, or murder, an appar-ently incredible performance for such a minute dose. Scientists cannot trace what happens to it in the body but can recognize its action by its results. On this analogy is it unreasonable to suppose that the human body has in it or can manufacture a substance so subtle that it cannot be detected with any of the present methods of examination, and yet so potent that in the form of radiation it can raise the human consciousness to such higher levels of cogni-tion where other planes of existence and other orders of being come into the range of perception of an individual?

What is of particular importance in this issue is the fact that the existence of this biochemical substance and its transformation into radiation, either as a natural measure or under the effect of certain practices and disciplines, is not to be taken purely on trust but can be observed and verified under the most rigid laboratory conditions in certain categories of men; and the observation can be repeated time after time until the Law is formally recognized. I am emphatic on this point on account of the fact, first, that I have myself observed the entire phenomenology of this experience for more than thirty years within myself and, second, the experience is confirmed not in a few but in hundreds upon hundreds of authentic documents dating from prehistoric times not only in India but in Tibet, China, Japan, and the Middle East also. The documentary evidence is so overwhelming that no reasonable man can disbelieve it even for a moment. Why it has not already created a revolution in modern thought is primarily due to the fact that many of these precious documents are written in what is known as Sandhya Bhasha, or twilight language, that is, in the cryptic form, which though plainly intelligible to one who has had the experience is often unintelligible to the noninitiate. With the elucidation that will be attempted in the works in hand on the subject, not only these enigmatical passages but also the veiled allusions to the changes resulting from an awakened Kundalini in the scriptures and other sacred lore of India will become readily understandable. Considering the volume of the ancient literature available on the subject in India alone, it would take a team of scholars several years to decipher the obscure writings even with the aid of the key furnished.

The question that now rises is how can the phenomena relating to Kundalini be demonstrated conclusively to meet the

87

demands of scientific research, even admitting that the documentary study can provide convincing material in their support? The answer to this question is simple, for it is precisely in this aspect of the problem that my own experience, though attended by awful suffering at times, has been of invaluable assistance to me, as if purposely designed to initiate a poor, mediocre man like me into the mystery. What my own experience has clearly revealed is the amazing fact that though guided by a Super-Intelligence, invisible but at the same time unmistakably seen conducting the whole operation, the phenomenon of Kundalini is entirely biological in nature. Probably no other spectacle, not even the most incredible supernormal performances of mystics and mediums, so clearly demonstrates the existence of an All-Pervading, Omniscient Intelligence behind the infinitely varied phenomena of life as the operations of a freshly awakened Kundalini. It is here that man for the first time becomes acutely aware of the staggering fact that this unimaginable Cosmic Intelligence is present at every spot in the Universe, and our whole personality—ego, mind, intellect, and all—is but an infinitely small bubble blown on this boundless Ocean; and to suppose that even a particle of this Ocean of Consciousness can ever become extinct or cease to be is more absurd than to imagine that there can be night on the sun. "From that lake (Ocean of Life) in which not even a mustard seed can find room (that has no dimensions)," says the Yogini Ialla, "all living creatures drink water (have their existence). From it deer, jackals, rhinoceros and sea-elephants (all forms of life) are born and into it they sink."

With the awakening of Kundalini, an amazing activity commences in the whole nervous system from the crown of the head to the toes. In Hatha Yoga, the activity coincides with the proficiency gained in Pranayama in the case of successful initiates, normally extremely few in number, but the operation is so gradual that it is hardly perceptible in the primary stages. In the case of those whose nervous systems have already attained a state of maturity, as a fruit of favorable heredity, the awakening can occur abruptly, whether effected by Raja Yoga or Hatha Yoga methods or by any other discipline, making use of concentration as the lever to achieve the aim. Whenever an awakening of this kind occurs, the normal biological rhythm of the body immediately experiences a drastic change, entirely beyond the power of control of the Sadhaka. His body is now transformed into a miniature laboratory, working at high speed day and night. In the Chinese documents this phenomenon is described as the "circulation of light" and in the Indian manuals as the "uprising of Shakti (life energy)." The nerves in all parts of the body, whose existence is never felt by the normal consciousness, are now forced by some invisible power to a new type of activity which either immediately or gradually becomes perceptible to the Sadhaka. Through all their innumerable endings, they begin to extract a nectar-like essence from the surrounding tissues, which, traveling in two distinct forms, one as radiation and the other as a subtle essence, streams into the spinal cord. A portion of the essence floods the reproductive organs which, too, become abnormally active as if to keep pace with the activity of the entire nervous system. The radiation, appearing as a luminous cloud in the head, streams into the brain and at the same time courses through the nerves, stimulating all the vital organs, especially the organs of digestion, to adjust their functions to the new life introduced into the system.

The awakening of Kundalini denotes, in other words, the phenomenon of rebirth, alluded to in plain or veiled terms in the religious lore of mankind. A more powerful and direct connection is now established between the individual and universal Consciousness, and the body, obeying implicitly new impulses and directions, communicated through Prana, the interconnecting biological medium, acting on itself, takes up an amazing process of rejuvenation, aimed to overhaul the nervous system and the brain, until a new type of consciousness or, in other words, a new inner man is born. The narration of the whole process would need a volume in itself and will be taken up in another work. It is sufficient to mention here that during the whole course of this transformation, in addition to the blood and other fuels present in the body, every particle of the powerful reproductive fluid in the system is sucked up through the spinal canal to irrigate and feed the various nerve junctions and the brain. This entirely biological operation is carried out in such an unmistakable way that even a novice in physiology cannot fail to notice it. The semen in men is now produced in such abundance that a tiny stream rises day and night through the spine into the cranium to provide the richest and the purest food for the now heavily overworked brain cells. In women, the sexual energy and secretions involved in erotics are used as the fuel. This is a perfect example of the forethought and the ingenuity of nature to keep the body equipped with all the necessities to make the completion of the evolutionary process, normally needing eons to accomplish, possible in the short span of one life. The tonic food provided by seminal essence, now manufactured in rich abundance and reaching every part of the brain with the cerebrospinal fluid, nourishes the brain cells and the nerve fibers, stimulating them to higher activity necessary for the emergence of a more enlarged consciousness than was manifested before.

This phenomenon of transformation or rebirth is alluded to by Christ in metaphorical language in his dialogue with Nicodemus when he says, "Verily, verily, I say unto thee, Except a man be born of water and of the Spirit, he cannot enter into the kingdom of God. That which is born of the flesh is flesh; and that which is born of the Spirit is spirit. Marvel not that I said unto thee, Ye must be born again." Among the Hindus the term "twice-born," applied to the higher castes, entitled to wear the sacred thread which has three strands, symbolic of the three nerve channels of Kundalini, only refers to the possibility of the same spiritual rebirth in them. It is amazing that a momentous concept on which the whole structure of the Hindu society was built in the Vedic age should have lost its true significance through the vicissitudes of time. The emphasis on chastity, or Brahmacharya, common to most religions, is clearly rooted in the fact that, in the case of earnest seekers after illumination, the need for the preservation of seed is imperative to meet the exigencies of the awakening. Viewed from any angle, the cult of Kundalini will be found to be the bedrock of all genuine religious experience, known in many parts of the earth to the spiritual adepts of the past. By a strange irony of fate, this vital knowledge is more scarce today, in this enlightened age, than in all the other periods of history. This is how nature retaliates to the arrogance of man.

There is an erroneous conception among certain ranks of scholars that transmuted seed is the direct cause of spiritual experience. As is readily understandable the human seed itself is built of two components: the gross organic substances and the subtle

Prana or Life-energy. About the latter we are entirely in the dark at this stage. This Prana is not the product of the reproductive machinery alone but is distilled from the whole body by the nerves. It is this pranic essence extracted by the nerves, countless in number, which, as a radiation, streams into the brain on the awakening of the Serpent Power. This more potent nerve and psychic energy, circulating in the system now, flows directly to the spinal cord and the brain, giving rise to the strange and weird phenomena that characterize the arousal of Kundalini in the initial stages. The grosser substances are used for the purpose of extra nourishment demanded by the cerebrospinal operation theater to carry the evolutionary processes to a successful termination. The unrestricted opportunity for sexual gratification allowed by nature to man has, it is obvious, a most important reason behind it. The precious organic substance and the concentrated energy, present in the seed, instead of being ejected for a momentary pleasure, can also be used, when the rejuvenation process is at work, as a tonic nourishment for the nerves and the brain cells in order to effect a metamorphosis of the inner man. By no other external feeding known to science can this wonderful transformation be brought about.

While it can be readily conceded that, with the present methods of observation, the transformation occurring in the consciousness of the initiate cannot be detected, even with the aid of mechanical devices, there can be absolutely no denial of the position that this is strictly a biological phenomenon. For instance, the intense activity of the sexual organs is clearly perceptible in the case of men. The ceaseless flow of the reproductive substances into the spinal cord, the vital organs, and the brain, and also the altered activity of the digestive system and even of the heart at times, can be easily observed with the help of the information available in the ancient literature on the subject.

The statements of the kind that during the process the shukra (semen) dries up with suction or becomes thin, that the male organ shrinks, or that the sexual appetite is lost, contained in the old manuals, cannot fail to convey important bits of information to the modern savants engaged in the investigation. An ancient Chinese work, *The Secret of the Golden Flower,* contains unmistakable hints about this process, which no one with some knowledge of the subject can fail to notice, and yet Jung, in his commentary on the book, entirely preoccupied with his own theories about the unconscious, despite the unambiguous nature of the statements in the work, finds in it only material for the corroboration of his own ideas and nothing beyond that. The same thing happened in a seminar held by him on Kundalini of which a written summary is still available in the Jung Institute. Not one of the savants present, as is evident from the views expressed by them, displayed the least knowledge about the real significance of this hoary cult and the tremendous import of the ancient doctrine they were discussing at the time.

IV.

THE MECHANISM OF EVOLUTION

IT IS EASY TO INFER THAT IF PARANORMAL ACHIEVEMENTS and a transcendental state of consciousness are possible for some men they must be possible for others also, provided the biological factors at the base of the manifestation, in the case of the former, are present in the latter too. It is impossible to believe that God or nature can be partial to those who possess the gifts and endow their minds with these extraordinary attributes as a mark of special favor. A more rational explanation for the phenomena, unless we choose to adopt a dogmatic attitude, would be to ascribe a biological cause for them and to find out by study and experiment where the secret lies. No one can deny that human consciousness itself is the expression of a biological organ and that, apart from the organism, it is never perceptible in any form. Is it not, therefore, but rational to assume that for any wide departure from the normal pattern of consciousness, there must occur a corresponding alteration in the biological machine also?

Fuel for normal activity of the human brain is not, as is sometimes supposed, supplied by blood alone. The real fuel of thought is the psychic energy supplied by a limited number of nerves after extracting it from various parts of the body. On the awakening of Kundalini the entire nervous system is soon harnessed to the task, with the result that a more powerful fuel, in the form of radiation, streams into the brain, enhancing its activity to such degree that a highly extended consciousness, which has an overwhelming effect on the initiate, now wafted to other planes of existence, replaces the old, narrow, sense-dominated awareness that never could rise beyond the strictly circumscribed limits.

The main hurdle in the way of an empirical demonstration of the change in consciousness lies in the fact that no method has yet been devised to determine the nature or potency of the psychic energy used by the brain. The moment this is achieved the verification of the subjective phenomena, as for instance the enlargement of consciousness, would also become possible. At the present moment we have absolutely no method to determine the variation in the nature of consciousness of a genius and a common man, though this difference both in the volume of awareness and the nature of the psychic energy used is always present.

Until the nature and properties of Life-energy, or *Prana*, serving as the fuel of thought, are determined by science, the modern savants will continue to be baffled by the phenomena of mind and consciousness in the same way as the ancients were mystified by the aurora borealis, lightning, thunder, and the like, until the mystery was solved by the discovery of electricity. The most practical way to study this elusive substance, more marvellous than any substance of the physical world, is to investigate the phenomenon of Kundalini. With the present highly developed methods of observation, once the clue is found it would not be difficult to follow the track with patience till conclusive data about the new field of research is collected. The domain of consciousness is, however, so amazing that there will be no cessation of mysteries and surprises for even the most powerful intellects till the end of time.

Positive evidence about the inner changes can, however, be furnished by the successful initiates themselves even at this stage. They have already done so in hundreds of memorable cases in India and other countries. These accounts can leave no one in doubt about the surpassing nature of the metamorphosis that is effected. The change occurring in the consciousness can never be imagined by one who has not had the experience. It is the stupendous nature of the vision which is at the root of the idea in the mind of a person who undergoes the experience that he is beholding a Superhuman Being, or a Superhuman state of Existence, surpassing everything he knows, including the whole universe. It is therefore no wonder that those who had the vision all through the past believed they were beholding the Creator Himself. During recent years Tennyson, Wordsworth, Proust, Bucke, and others had experiences somewhat similar to those of mystics, under different circumstances, without undergoing those rigorous disciplines usually associated with spiritual unfoldment. When regular research is started, it will be found that also in the past this "gratuitous grace" has been a common feature of mystical experience, as if those who had it were already fashioned for it from birth or needed but a slight stimulus to gain it.

The extremely diversified accounts of religious experience are due to the variation in the mental level, ideas, and cultural development of those who have it. For a thorough investigation of the phenomenon it is necessary that a team of scholars and scientists, comprising skeptics and believers both, should take up a course of exercises for a sufficient period in a spirit of dedication, as is done for other scientific objectives, with due regard to the ethical standards necessary for it. And then they could evaluate the results.

Even one case of awakening would be sufficient to determine the biological nature of the phenomenon, and to observe the various changes and developments that occur. The metabolic processes of the body are highly accelerated, and an inner process of brain building and streamlining, somewhat akin to the processes occurring in an embryo in the womb, takes place until consciousness is completely transmogrified and a superior type of mind is born. What achievements are not possible with an awakened Kundalini, once the feasibility of the transformation is empirically demonstrated and the biological factors involved become known to the men of science? It can be readily imagined to what levels of perception the brain can be raised when it is constantly fed, during the process of renovation, by the most powerful nerve food not obtainable by any other means, prepared by the reproductive organs in amazing abundance under the impact of a newly generated activity completely unknown to science.

It is not at all necessary to depend entirely on the accounts of those under discipline about the inner changes experienced by them. There are unmistakable external signs also by which these changes can be detected and even measured. When transformed, the initiate must become a genius or a virtuoso of a high order, with extraordinary power of expression, both in verse and prose, or extraordinary artistic talents. Some of the ancient prophets and seers are the historical examples of this metamorphosis. Precognition, powers of healing, psychic talents, and other miraculous gifts may develop simultaneously along with genius. A modern intellectual with a healthy constitution and noble attributes of character can bloom into a spiritual prodigy, a man of such extraordinary gifts and talents that he can shine as an idol before the admiring eyes of the multitudes, with a power of fascination and appeal possessed only by the most magnetic of men. In this way the metamorphosis effected can bear striking testimony to the efficacy of processes generated by Kundalini. I am making these statements with full responsibility about the accuracy of what I say, and there are countless volumes to support my assertions in every detail. The explanation for the metamorphosis is not hard to accept. The evolutionary mechanism is so constructed that at a certain state of maturity it can be stimulated to such intense activity by means of appropriate methods that the evolutionary cycle can be completed in one's lifetime, raising man to the next higher stage of consciousness decreed for him by Divine Ordination.

There is absolutely no difficulty in a scientific investigation of the phenomenon when the spheres of its operation are known. The biological reactions in the body are unmistakable. The ceaseless suction of the seminal fluid and its flow into the spinal canal, nerve junctions of the vital organs, and the brain cannot remain undetected. The symbol of an erect organ of generation in some statues of deities in India is indicative of Urdhava-retas, or of this upward streaming of the reproductive essence for effecting transformation of consciousness. The phenomenon is so ancient and so widespread that it is amazing that modern science has no inkling of it even now. The halo or aureola shown round the heads or figures of saints and illumined sages is symbolic of the inner illumination experienced in the metamorphosis of consciousness. There is a noticeable change in the digestive and excretory functions of the body during the course of the transformation.

There are other developments that can be pointed out to the investigators when a research project is taken in hand. It is obvious that from both the subjective and objective sides, the phenomenon is as possible of verification as any other function of the human body. The point that now rises is why should such an overwhelming importance be attached to this research, when the ultimate object of the awakening of Kundalini is merely a change in consciousness which, as the past record shows, can be effective only in an extremely limited number of cases, and therefore the phenomenon cannot be of importance or interest for the whole of the human race? The futility of the question becomes obvious when we recollect what giant revolutions in human life and thought were effected by the handful of spiritual geniuses born in different parts of the earth during the historical period. This factor alone presents a phenomenon of such magnitude that it makes research on Kundalini a pressing need of the times. But there are many other equally important factors which when taken together make Kundalini virtually the arbiter of human destiny and, for that reason, by far the most powerful driving influence on the life of man.

Another important factor in this series is the decisive role played by Kundalini in providing an avenue for the satisfaction of the deep-rooted religious impulse in man. We are all aware of the fact that the urge to experience the transcendental or to solve the riddle of our being is, to a more or less extent, present in most men, and in some cases it assumes such an overwhelming proportion that it becomes the most powerful guiding influence in life. Even the skeptics are not without the desire to solve the mystery of creation. But no attempt made by the intellect, assisted by all the inventions of science, can penetrate the veil, because the veil itself is the creation of the intellect. It is only by self-transcendence that light begins to penetrate into the darkness, dissolving the problem, as shadows melt at the approach of dawn.

This elevation of consciousness can only occur through the transformations brought by Kundalini and by no other agency human or divine. The present rapid multiplication of sects and creeds, which the orthodox custodians of the various faiths are powerless to stop or even to account for, owes its origin to the mounting pressure on the brain caused by the religious urge, the inevitable fruit of civilization and leisure, which only an awakened Kundalini can ease. The millions upon millions of men and women who seek solace in occult practices of any kind, in Yoga, in drugs, in prayer and worship or in any other form of spiritual effort and eagerly hunt for teachers and adepts for guidance are, often without knowing it, yielding to a subconscious urge to rouse Kundalini, an urge almost as powerful as that which makes a healthy young woman long for a child. Even in the Communist countries in the next few decades, the ever-increasing pressure of the inexorable evolutionary processes will break the fetters forged by a political ideology, ignorant of the law, that suppresses healthy expression of the religious impulse and, if this outflow is still denied, may result in the same violence in finding a vent as was previously used to prevent it. History will follow in the reverse direction unless the Law is recognized and obeyed.

Let us now come to another equally important aspect of Kundalini. With all the knowledge provided by modern psychology at our disposal, we are now in a position to guess correctly what can be the outcome of denial, suppression, or distortion of a deep-rooted natural impulse present in the mind of man. We are already aware of the unwholesome effects caused by the denial or suppression of other deep-rooted natural tendencies, like the reproductive urge and the maternal instinct. On this analogy would it be wrong to suppose that the same results can follow from the suppression or denial of the religious impulse and that they too can lead to mental unrest, depression, perversion, disorder in the system, abnormal behavior, and in extreme cases to insanity?

Since Kundalini is the fountainhead of the religious desire in man, it means that a mode of life and conduct or a system of society that puts a brake on its legitimate activity can never be conducive to peace and happiness but must, on the other hand, lead to psychic and physiological disturbances both in the individual and in the group. The religious impulse, unlike the reproductive urge, is not static but dynamic in its operations. In other words, it is not appeased by the same kind of nourishment over and over again but demands a change in diet, according to the evolutionary stature and the intellectual acumen gained, and when this is denied it gropes blindly for other vicarious foods to satisfy the hunger gnawing inside. The multiplicity of creeds in this age is, therefore, nothing to be wondered at. The tendency will continue to spread until the right food is found.

Mental disturbance and psychosis are, at the present state of our knowledge about this nerve mechanism, not infrequently the possible consequences of a sudden arousal of Kundalini. This possibility has always been recognized by the specialists in this science. In the ancient pictorial representations, the Goddess is always shown making the sign of dispelling fear with one of her hands. Fear is one of the most common symptoms of neuroses and psychotic conditions. The initiation ceremonies in India and Tibet and the hideous practices, such as sitting astride a corpse for meditation, resorted to in some cases, are merely crude methods to fortify the mind of the initiates against the unimaginably frightful phases of the awakening. It should not be difficult to understand that the practices aimed to arouse the Serpent Power sometimes result in abruptly forcing open the central channel and the connected compartment in the brain at a time when the system is not yet attuned to such a development. In such cases terrible ordeals await the initiates, through which only some survive. It is easy to imagine that rapid flights to higher levels of consciousness, as is envisaged in every form of Yoga, cannot be without some degree of risk—unless the mind and body have been attuned to them by appropriate methods, including proper cultivation of the will power—for seekers who take to them with all the earnestness at their command.

Taking now another feature of religion, we find, as I have pointed out in the opening lines of this book, that primitive religions were a bundle of superstition, revolting forms of worship, savage ritual, and myth. Since the evolutionary impulse is a part and parcel of the psychosomatic organism of man, and not any miraculous influence exerted by God in chosen cases nor a thought wave created by any prophet, it is only natural that the expression of the impulse should correspond to the psychological level of the people. Therefore we should not expect the religion of the barbarian and the savage to have that refinement and sublimity that permeated throughout the historical period of the civilized nations. And yet at the same time we cannot expect that the religious concepts and ideas prevalent thousands of years ago would continue to hold the same attraction and appeal for a higher intellectual level of people. Revolt in some form against the obsolete ideas and forms of worship or ritual is, therefore, just a natural outcome of the psycho-mental evolution of the race. The inexorable march of time must cause the same revolutions in the spiritual sphere as it has caused and is causing in the social and political fields to conform to the evolutionary needs of mankind. All cramping influences can only prolong the agony of resistance to an unavoidable advancing tide. The mushrooming growth of countless novel cults and creeds is indicative of the first impact of the tide and the eager search of the masses for a more satisfying spiritual food than the one provided by the older faiths.

We now come to the most important aspect of Kundalini. It can be readily understood that the evolutionary impulse cannot be active only in the individuals but must be operative in a collective sense as well. The influence of evolutionary processes on the ecological development of a whole species or group is now clearly recognized by the biologists. It is obvious that in order to meet the needs of the evolutionary growths, changes in the environment—social, political, and moral—would be necessary from time to time to meet the demands of the developing psychomental fabric of the individuals and of the race too. Where this adjustment is delayed, causing a retardation in growth, revolts, revolutions, and wars intervene to effect, with widespread suffering and bloodshed, what could have been achieved by peaceful means provided the underlying Law were known and its mode of operation understood. Constant violation of the Law and the prevalence of social, moral, and political conditions not in conformity with the evolutionary needs must, at last, lead to ceaseless turmoil, senescence, and decay. The ancient civilizations, cultures, and empires, after attaining a certain level of ascendancy, fell victims to decadence as the lives of the people did not conform to those standards—political, moral, and social—that were demanded by the mental stature attained as the fruit of evolution at the time they touched the zenith of their career. The sudden or gradual eclipse of the ascendant nations of the last few centuries was also brought about by the same causes. The degenerative tendencies that have now set in among almost the whole of mankind as the consequence of modern defective ways of life, incommensurate with the present evolutionary stature of the race, owe their origin to the same factors. No amenities provided by science, no new spate of inventions, no psychological cures, and no amount of education can arrest the growth of this canker unless the evolutionary demands are fulfilled. The danger to the race from a continued neglect of these conditions in the present state of technological development is too plain to escape the notice of even the least observant. But the reason why effective measures are not employed to end it, is that the present habits of thought have become too ingrained to be changed, a last symptom of decay.

It is a historical fact that all the founders of the existing major faiths of mankind and all great prophets, mystics, and seers, who claimed to have won access to Divinity in one form or the other, were almost all of them men and women of extraordinary intellectual acumen, and most of them were credited with the possession of the miraculous gifts of prophecy, clairvoyance, control over the elements, healing power, and the like. It is also well known that miraculous powers have always been associated with prophets and saints from prehistoric times, and even in this age the general belief is that accomplished Yogis, saints, and other spiritual men in some way gain contact with and even power of control over the subtle forces of nature, beyond the reach of common men. We have already seen that the high-potency psychic radiation, produced by Kundalini from the marvellous chemical laboratory of the human body, is the common source of all the supernormal states of consciousness common to prophets, seers, and mystics of all categories. Since genius, high intellectual calibre, and miraculous gifts are a common adornment of the mystic mind, it is but logical to conclude that genius and miraculous powers also owe their origin to the operations of Kundalini. From this it follows that the highest intellectual and artistic talent (such as in the case of men of genius and virtuosos—and psychic or miraculous powers, in the case of mediums and sensitives or others possessing the gift of healing or other psi faculties without the visionary state of consciousness peculiar to mystics and seers) also flow from the same source. In actual fact, this phenomenon provides valuable circumstantial evidence in support of the stand that Kundalini is the evolutionary energy and mechanism in man. It is only a process of evolution that can lead to the extraordinary formations of the brain biologically necessary for the exhibition of talents and gifts entirely beyond the capacity of normal brains. Taking into consideration the transformation that has been wrought in every sphere of human life and thought by a few hundred talented and gifted men, through all of history, can there be any line of research more important and more beneficial for humankind than that which would show the way to tap the amazing source that showers these priceless gifts, thereby making cultivation of genius a practicable achievement for man?

The question that arises here, as a natural sequence of what has been stated, is that if the Serpent Power is the source behind genius and high intellectual or artistic talents it must also be the factor responsible for the evil geniuses of history, the highly talented military commanders, dictators, and demagogues who drenched humanity in blood, and also for the human monsters who, dead to every moral sentiment, with their proclivity and genius for crime, commit such dreadful acts which make the horrified readers of their gruesome exploits shiver with fright. This is the malignant or destructive aspect of Kundalini, symbolized by the ancient Indian savants in the form of Kali, who, black in color from head to foot, is depicted with her mouth dripping with human blood, a severed human head in one of her hands and a garland of skulls round her neck. In her benign form Kundalini is Durga, the creatrix, the dispeller of ignorance and all evils and ills. In her malignant form she is Kali, the Goddess of destruction, often the tutelary deity of those engaged in nefarious activities, thugs, dacoits, black magicians, and the like. It is incredible that a vital secret concerning the existence of a biological device in the human body that has the capacity to raise man to the stature of a god, with supernormal gifts and virtues, like saviours and sages, or the capacity to fashion him into a monster, as in the case of the human scourges of the past and present, which has been known in India for centuries, should still be a sealed book to the luminaries of this age. It is this ignorance of an awful secret of nature that has exposed mankind to the horror of terrible wars, revolutions, inhuman suffering, and shattering loss during the current century. No amount of material wealth and prosperity can save mankind from the depredations committed by highly gifted, amoral men, pursuing ambitious goals, in whom Kundalini is awake in a malignant form. Their hold over the masses being irresistible, their power of organization unmatched, and their military skill unequalled, even one specimen of this class, in the present state of technological knowledge, can play havoc with the whole of humanity and all it has achieved during the last many thousand years.

The only silver lining in the dark clouds threatening mankind at present is the recognition by science, after a thorough investigation, of this almighty Law. The race can no longer afford (now or in the decades to come) to play with fire and allow her own ignorance of the awful Law to result in the continued birth of evil geniuses, fatal to the survival of the race. The point now arises as to how a divine power, designed to lead the race to unimaginable heights of glory, peace, and happiness in the outer world and to transcendental states of consciousness in the inner, can be so diverted from its natural course that it produces virtual monsters for the destruction and torment of the race. The answer to this very relevant question is not hard to find. It is the ignorance of the Law and the lack of cooperation on the part of the surface consciousness with the hidden operations of the evolutionary force that are at the bottom of the catastrophe. All the Revelations made by the known prophets of the past, to a more or less extent, contain precious hints about the ways of life to be followed to avoid resistance to or obstruction in the process of evolution which, as always happens in the case of violations of any natural law, can be disastrous both for the individual and the race. It is very well known that man needs a certain complete and balanced diet to insure freedom from disease and a smooth, efficient functioning of the system. For the purpose of proper, harmonious growth of the body and the mind nature provides a ready-made, easily digestible food for the human infant, complete in all respects in the mother's breasts. In the same way, the transformative processes of Kundalini need a certain healthy and harmonious condition of the body and the mind to compound in proper proportions the subtle essences that form the fuel for the high-potency psychic radiation which is at the bottom of all extraordinary or supernormal exhibitions of the human mind.

A wrong mode of life, disharmonious social and political environments, improper food and drink, immoderation and intemperance, and also excessive worry, anxiety, and fear, unrestricted ambition and desire, greed, selfishness, envy, jealousy, and hatred, in fact all those attributes of mind that have been condemned as evil by the revealed knowledge of mankind, acting adversely on the system, interfere directly with the proper manufacture of the precious fuels, with the result that the psychic radiation, lacking healthy nourishment, takes on a stunted, distorted, or diseased form, in the same way that lack of proper food in insufficient measure stunts, distorts, or damages the health of a suckling babe. This is the reason why Revelation came to guide mankind. Like the nature of the Law, its enormous implications and effects were and are even now unknown. Every prophet and seer born on earth came, in fact, knowingly or unknowingly to draw attention to this occult Law. The signs and symptoms of degeneration that we notice now, and which marked the closing phases of all the premier civilizations and victorious empires of the past, point conclusively to a deterioration in the physical and mental assets of a people or nation, causing an impoverishment in the quality of the evolving psychic energy, leading to those deficiencies, faults, and flaws which are characteristic of decadence in the rising generations and those yet unborn. Decline in moral values, family affection, conjugal love, or in the ideas of loyalty and fidelity or the standards of truth, honesty, patience, and perseverance, absence of originality, lack of the sense of responsibility and self-restraint, intemperance, immoderation, and indolence are some of the characteristics of the decadent mind.

Disproportion, deformation, or distortion in the psychic radiation is the cause of the appearance of not only the sadistic geniuses, who cause horrible slaughters from time to time, but also of many forms of neurosis and insanity. Professor Zaehner in his book, *Mysticism, Sacred and Profane,* has touched a very important point in citing the instance of John Custance, a certified manic-depressive, who is prone to mystical experiences during his manic-periods. Similarly Huxley in his work, *Heaven and Hell,* has cited the case of Renée, a schizophrenic who has given an autobiographical account of her own passage through madness. She calls the world of the schizophrenic "the country of lit-upness," as Huxley writes, of which the illumination for her is infernal—an intense electric glare without a shadow, ubiquitous and implacable. The summer sunshine is malignant, and so on. The subject is too vast to be dealt with in this short summary, but from my own experience and from a study of many cases that I have come across, both in India and in the West, it is obvious that the awakening of Kundalini in a person not well adjusted to it, with defective organs or an unhealthy nervous system or a faulty heredity or any other flaw, which research will disclose, leads to hysterical, neurotic, or insane conditions of the mind. The liability to mental disorder in the case of those who take to Yoga or other forms of religious discipline is recognized both in India and in the Middle East. Those who stumble on the path and survive with some form of mental derangement are caller "Mastanas" in Persian, as opposed to "Farzanas" of the sober class. Psychotics of this category in their lucid intervals exhibit clairvoyance or other paranormal faculties despite their abnormal behavior at other times. I have come across several cases of enlargement of consciousness in Europe, arising from an active Kundalini. Some of them, though possessing lofty traits of character and even, at times, psychic gifts, because of an unfavorable environment or other reasons are variable in their moods, and instead of experiencing that spontaneous ever-abiding joy which a gracious Kundalini bestows, also pass through periods of depression. The growing flood of mental troubles, which is a curse of modern civilization even among the more advanced nations, is nature's forewarning that the evolutionary process is going wrong. The relation of schizophrenia to puberty in a vast majority of cases has a special connotation in the light of what I say.

It is not necessary for me to emphasize the paramount importance of the disclosures I am making. I have presented this summary to make the enormous implications of the doctrine of Kundalini clear beyond doubt, as I have found by experience that even among the intellectuals only a very few, blessed with intuition, have been able to grasp them in their entirety. What I emphatically assert is that one single Law is at the base of all, at the present moment, inexplicable phenomena of the human mind. Only one remarkable series of changes, caused in the psychic energy that serves as fuel for thought, is responsible for all the varied and complex phenomena that present at this time insolvable riddles to science. The greater incidence of insanity among the men of genius and the seeds of eccentricity in many of them (considered in the light of the fact that the danger of madness is ever present in any effort directed to arouse the

Serpent Power) clearly establishes the existence of a common link between the two. Research into Kundalini implies, in fact, an investigation into almost all, at the moment, obscure phenomena of the mind.

The investigation carried out by the Society for Psychical Research and other allied groups or individuals on mediums, sensitives, clairvoyants, psychic healers, Yoga practitioners and the like has not yet been proved conclusive, for the reason that in this way the investigation is directed to the innumerable branches and leaves of a giant tree of which the root is Kundalini. It is far more practicable to take hold of the root to make a study of the phenomenon than to examine the branches and leaves to find a solution to a problem that becomes a hundred times more intricate there. In dealing with mind and consciousness we deal with a different type of energy and a different plane of existence than that known to us through our senses. It is a recognition of this fact that is decisive in launching a research into the occult. This is the base from which a real study of the cosmos begins, for the universe we see is real only in the human state of consciousness. Beyond that it is reduced to a mirage in the dimension just one step higher to it, denoting the tremendous difference caused by a change in the potency of the psychic radiation effected by Kundalini.

Although I am as sure of the fact that all the numerous developments I have mentioned proceed from the working of Kundalini, that is, from the operation of one, single, at the moment hidden Law of nature, ruling the world of life, as I am of my own existence, yet I must say with all the emphasis at my command that every word I have said should be first weighed in the scale of reason, then rubbed on the touchstone of the recorded experiences of the past, and finally tested in the crucible of research before the least credence is placed on it. I say so because a single false doctrine, widely accepted by the unwary, can at this stage do incalculable damage to human weal. One single Law, as I have said, is at the root of almost all the inexplicable phenomena, urges, and impulses of the human mind, as for instance the impulse to worship, superstition, desire for supernatural or spiritual experience, the awe of the numinous, belief in the supermundane and the hereafter, supernormal faculties—precognition, clairvoyance, telepathy, prenatal memory, automatism, mental healing and the like, intuition, skill in astrology, palmistry, fortune-telling, etc., genius, mystical experience, revelation, inspiration, neurosis, insanity, moral sense, aesthetics, piety, the rise and fall of nations, degeneration in individuals, families, and groups, evolution and its allied phenomena—all proceed from the operation of but one cosmic Law. From this it is obvious that the Law of Parsimony operates with equal force in the realm of the spirit also. And how could it be otherwise, for all the universe we see and all the law and order we perceive in it are but reflections of a plane of existence compared to which the sensory world dwindles to the likeness of a thin vapor floating across the surface of an ever-lasting, ever-bright, limitless sun. All extraordinary and supernormal psychic gifts, all extraordinary and abnormal conditions of the mind, all the desire for transcendental experience or for the vision of God or for a nobler and happier state of being, and all the revolutionary ideas, both good and bad, flow from altered conditions of the psychic radiation, produced by Kundalini, as both light and darkness proceed from altered positions of the rotating earth.

V.

THE DIVINE POSSIBILITIES IN MAN

CHOSEN BY DESTINY, THAT RULES EVERY EVENT OF THE UNIVERSE, to make this fresh disclosure of an already discovered superphysical Law, in a manner incomprehensible to myself, because of my own limitations and human frailties, I do my utmost to draw the attention of the scholars of this age to the vital importance of a scientific investigation of the phenomenon. I know that the yet imperfect and incomplete account of this divine mechanism I have rendered in my writings can only kindle a spark in the darkness of doubt and confusion prevailing at present; but at the same time, I am confident that the labor and sacrifice of those men of science who, unconvinced by the existing theories about mind, are following like sleuths the trail toward a real solution to the problem and those individuals who, prompted by a divine impulse, are striving day and night for a purer and better world, will succeed in establishing the existence of the almighty power mechanism of Kundalini, as described by me, to the satisfaction of one and all. In answer to the question that the divulgence of the secret of this awful Power might place in the hands of the wicked a terrible weapon to harm the world, it is enough to point out that save for the born cases, the arousal of Kundalini in one whose mind harbors evil will invariably lead to insanity or death. An open knowledge of the secret can act as the surest safeguard against the misuse of the august Power because at least the well-informed section of mankind will have been sufficiently educated to distinguish a diabolic product of this kind, however eloquent and magnetic he might be.

I stand alone in the disclosures that I am making. There is every likelihood that both from the sides of religion and science eyebrows will be raised and open doubts expressed at what I say. This will be only a transitory phase, as every important discovery in the realm of knowledge almost invariably took the world by surprise. But when the destined hour arrives, circumstances so transpire that, however incredible the disclosure might have appeared in the beginning, soon after a day comes when it becomes the most talked about topic of the day. In my humble view there is nothing that can counteract the overhanging threat of nuclear holocaust like the knowledge of Kundalini. Once the possibility of a spiritual rebirth with the arousal of this mighty Power is accepted by mankind, Kundalini Yoga will provide the most sublime enterprise for the pure-minded and intelligent adventurous spirits of the age. To the share of this lofty class of men, adorned with the knowledge of the inner and the outer worlds, will fall the herculean task of educating humanity in the essentials of this almighty spiritual Law to guide the race to the glorious estate ordained for it.

There can be nothing more antagonistic to the lofty concept of Divinity, as inculcated by most of the religions of mankind, than the idea that at any time in his long career on earth mortal man can attain to a state where he will have gained all the knowledge about the creation and the Absolute. The moment he begins to think in this vein he arrogates to himself a position of rivalry to the omniscient Creator of the Universe, a mark of arrogance which his knowledge of the physical universe should have driven out of his head long ago. Those who oppose a new idea or a new wave of thought without allowing it a fair trial clearly betray the presence of a lurking idea in their minds, born of pride, that they know all that can be known of the world. I, therefore, beseech all those who strive for a happy future for mankind, both from the ranks of scholars and men of faith, to put what I have said to the severest possible test they choose in the experiments conducted to prove the correctness of the hypothesis.

About the methods of awakening Kundalini, the precautions needed and the way of life to be followed by those who would like to offer themselves for this sublime enterprise, a good deal of information is already contained in the ancient manuals and some more would be added in the volumes that will appear on the subject from time to time. It is, however, necessary to point out that the present wave to equate mystical experience with the hallucinatory conditions caused by certain drugs or with hypnotic conditions induced by suggestion, guided meditation, or multisensory sound and light environments or by any other artificial means is the outcome of a most erroneous conception about the genuine mystical state. Resort to these artificial conditions, demanding no effort at self-mastery, is as dangerous to the evolutionary development of the human brain as the use of narcotic drugs by ascetics has been to the spiritual cause in India. Until the law behind mystical phenomena is established, attempts to imitate conditions of consciousness about which nothing definite is yet known can only be treated as apish. These methods have been employed from time immemorial to satisfy the itch of minds ravenously hungry for spiritual experience but whose mode of life and attributes of character stand in the way of real self-unfoldment. They are like the sweets containing opiates, used by unscrupulous nurses sometimes to put restless children entrusted to their care to sleep. The very idea of gaining access to God by means of chemicals, mental suggestion, or some meditational technique constitutes a mockery of all the sublime teachings of religion that call on man to prepare himself for the supreme vision by adherence to lofty ideals of life. Those men of science and those teachers of spiritual disciplines who overlook this vital point in this way express denial of the need for moral elevation and ennoblement in those who strive for spiritual enlightenment.

The finished products of Kundalini must transcend the normal limits of the human brain. If this transcendence does not occur, the visionary experiences are either a delusion or a myth. Even those who have sporadic glimpses of the Ineffable but for a few times in their life are usually men of genius or of high intellectual stature. Those in a state of perennial ecstasy must essentially have uncommon intellectual talents, paranormal gifts, and

117

an altered rhythm of the nervous system. In their case the enlarged consciousness persists even in slumber, for which reason
such sleep is called "Yoga Nidra" or the sleep of Yoga. The marvellous Power Reservoir of Kundalini, the unmistakable symbol
of the Divine in man, opens up new horizons of such sublimity,
joy, and glory that even a modest description would appear incredible unless a few transformed adepts support my assertions
to convince scholars of the golden future ordained for humanity.
In no other period in history have the learned been so mistrustful
of the divine possibilities in man as they are now, and in no other
age has the need for spiritual geniuses been so urgent as it is at
this time.

The human mind is so constituted that no luxury and no
treasure of the earth can assuage its burning fever seeking an
explanation for its own existence. All the heavy weight of this
inscrutable mystery, all the questions posed by intellect, all the
suffering of the harrowing ascent of evolution, all the pain felt
at the injustice and misery prevailing in the world, all the dis-
appointment of shattered dreams and broken hopes, all the
anguish of eternal partings from near and dear ones, and all the
fear of ill health, decay, and death—vanish like vapor at the rise of
the inner Sun, at the recognition of the inmost Self, beyond
thought, beyond doubt, beyond pain, beyond mortality which,
once perceived, illumines the darkness of the mind as a flash
of strong lightning cleaves the darkness of the night, leaving man
transformed with but one glimpse of the inexpressible splendor
and glory of the spiritual world. May this sublime knowledge
become accessible to all. May there come enlightenment and
peace to the minds of all.